Evolving as a Digital Schol

Teaching and Researching in a Digital World

Evolving as a Digital Scholar

Teaching and Researching in a Digital World

Wim Van Petegem,
JP Bosman,
Miné De Klerk,
and Sonja Strydom

LEUVEN UNIVERSITY PRESS

Published with the support of
KU Leuven Fund for Fair Open Access

Published in 2021 by Leuven University Press / Presses Universitaires de Louvain /
Universitaire Pers Leuven. Minderbroedersstraat 4, B-3000 Leuven (Belgium).

ISBN 978 94 6270 278 3 (Paperback)
ISBN 978 94 6166 390 0 (ePDF)
ISBN 978 94 6166 391 7 (ePUB)
https://doi.org/10.11116/9789461663900
D/2021/1869/39
NUR: 070

Layout: Crius Group
Cover design: Frederik Danko
Cover illustration: Muhkzihajj Sembiring/Shutterstock.com

Contents

Acknowledgments

Many people have contributed with ideas, advice, comments, suggestions and support, before and during the development of this book:

- ✓ The organisers of the ADA African Doctoral Academy at Stellenbosch University, and the VLIR-UOS who financed the AVLM training, for giving us the opportunity during several consecutive years to build up our knowledge in this domain and to experiment with our Digital Scholar framework.
- ✓ The participants of our workshops, both ADA and AVLM, for listening to us, for being so active in the sessions (and later), for providing us with feedback and for helping us further to shape our training materials and activities.
- ✓ The leadership of our universities, for granting us space and time to engage in workshops and trainings as part of our academic work, and for supporting international exchange, which the collaboration between the authors stems from.
- ✓ The colleagues, in our own universities and many others, for inspiring us with their stories, for sharing their insights, for being guest lecturers in our workshops, for discussing preliminary versions of the contents of this book, for challenging us with their questions, and for helping us in developing learning materials.
- ✓ A special thank you to Lucille Müller, Multimedia Designer at the Centre for Learning Technologies, Stellenbosch University, for her graphic design work in this book.
- ✓ The peer reviewers, Michael Rowe and Dick Ng'ambi, for being our critical friends, for commenting on the first draft of our manuscript and for suggesting additions, deletions or changes in the text, always in a very constructive way.
- ✓ The publisher Leuven University Press, and especially our editor, Mirjam Truwant, for believing in our project, for offering professional help throughout the whole writing process, and for continuing to stimulate us and meet all requirements to make this book project happen.

✓ The KU Leuven Fund for Fair Open Access, for allowing us to publish this manuscript as an open access e-book, affordable and easy to read online, download, print and copy by a large audience around the globe.
✓ The future readers of this book, for going on a journey with us and, hopefully, for letting us know how they evolve as Digital Scholars.

There is no way this book would be possible without the valuable help of all of you. Many, many thanks!

Foreword

Why this book?

With a title like 'Evolving as a Digital Scholar' one could wonder why we are writing a book about this topic. Shouldn't we better go for a digital publication, somewhere on the web, quicker to adapt to new evolutions in the field, and easier to access for readers across the globe? Well, apparently there is a need for a more tangible artefact in book format (on top of electronic resources) that people can use as a reference when they have heard us, the authors, speaking about digital scholarship in our workshops. That's indeed what we have experienced in the last decade after having been involved in frequent workshops, both in our own institutions and elsewhere. Participants (mostly scholars, and by now 'digital' scholars) expect to return to their daily academic life with a manual or handbook (either on paper or in an e-book format) where the principles of what has been explained and practised in the workshop is written down in such a way that they can refer back to it later whenever there is a reason for (as a rehearsal, as inspiration, as food for thought, as basis for their own workshops, etc.).

As instructors in those training sessions, and as digital scholars ourselves, we build our professional learning offerings on the existing knowledge base (and our own experiences, of course). To the best of our knowledge however this is a unique book, although some other authors address similar topics and come close to ours. Their work is of a sometimes more conceptual, theoretical nature, while this book is still evidence-based, though more a hands-on, practical book. Others deal with particular aspects of academic life, like teaching or researching, while we are addressing all roles of an academic or, better, a scholar (who is not just a teacher or a researcher). Some other books focus on certain digital technologies, like social media or web services, while we go broader in digital technologies, covering not only audio-visual media, multimedia and social media, but also webtools, apps, devices, infrastructure, etc. Sometimes one can find books examining the relation between digital technology and the academic world, on the level of higher education in general and the institution as an organisation, while our focus is more on the individual scholar (working in higher education). In sum we believe that this book clearly sheds a unique light on what could be understood as digital scholarship and how one can evolve as a digital scholar in all its aspects.

Where does this book come from?

As already indicated, this book draws on our experiences in many workshops we have been involved in, as individual instructors/academic developers but also as a team, which has brought a more global perspective into those workshops and courses, and hence this book is written together. It is worthwhile mentioning here that there are mainly two distinct initiatives that form the basis of this book. On the one hand, there is the *AVLM-training*. AVLM stands for Audio-visual Learning Materials, since the original focus of the training was on the production of audio-visual learning materials. Later on, the scope has enlarged, and the title and acronym no longer corresponded with the content of the training, but it is known under this name and we keep it as such. This training was funded by VLIR-UOS.[1] It is an intensive eight-week programme in Flanders (Belgium) that enhances the skills and competences of academic and educational support staff of institutions in the South in the field of new educational technologies. More than 10 editions with each time between 12 and 18 participants from all continents in the South have been organised at KU Leuven since early 2000. The second series of workshops we build upon is *The Digital Scholar* course. This is a one-week professional learning opportunity in the ADA[2] (African Doctoral Academy) at Stellenbosch University. Since 2017, this workshop has been organised twice a year for groups of between 8 and 15 participants, and since the COVID-19 pandemic, also in a virtual format. Other learning opportunities offered by us in different countries further enrich the book and add to its intercultural flavour.

It was during the first visit to Stellenbosch University in 2014 by one of the authors, Wim Van Petegem, that the idea popped up to work on something together, an article, a massive open online course (MOOC), or maybe something totally different. It all came to us quite unexpectedly in the end. Sometime later, at the occasion of a reciprocal exchange of another author, JP Bosman, to KU Leuven, we were sitting together trying to design a course that incorporates digital technologies into the world of the higher education practitioner. It was towards the end of the staff mobility exchange, and we were getting worried that our time together was running out. We intuitively knew what we wanted to do as experienced digitally fluent practitioners, but the why, what and how were still evading us. Sitting across our desks we were talking in circles, until we started making notes and drawing pictures on the desk pad on the table between us. "JP, what we need is a framework!" The notes and ideas started flowing and then, suddenly, the puzzle pieces started making sense. It was quite a euphoric feeling when a meaningful structure emerged which became the core idea for the later *The Digital Scholar* course. That is how this book was born!

From the first idea for a book to finally publishing this first edition was a long but rewarding journey. With four authors from two universities, we were lucky to have collaborated before in the workshops. That gave us enough common background on the contents we wanted to cover in this book, but also, and above all, the trust we needed to work together as a team of authors. We decided from the beginning that each of us would take full responsibility for two chapters in the book, and we would allow a personal touch in these chapters, so no final editing was intended to streamline the style or approach taken by the individual authors in their chapters. However, we discussed in several (virtual and face-to-face) meetings draft versions of our chapters, as critical friends. In iterative rounds we have read the work by the others, in order to adhere to the chosen common structure, to make the book comprehensive and avoid overlap, and to align our own personal writing style as much as possible to a spontaneously created team's writing style. All this has led to the book you now have in your hands or are reading on your screen.

What to expect in this book?

This manual explains how digitally agile scholars can comfortably navigate the digital world of today and tomorrow. It foregrounds three key domains of digital agility: getting involved in research, education and (community) service, mobilising (digital) skills on various levels, and acting in multiple roles, both individually and interlinked with others.

After an introduction that outlines the foundations of this three-dimensional framework, the chapters focus on different roles and skills associated with evolving as a digital scholar. There is the author, who writes highly specialised texts for expert peers; the storyteller, who crafts accessible narratives for a broader audience in the form of blogs or podcasts; the creator, who uses graphics, audio, and video to motivate audiences to delve deeper into the material; the integrator, who develops and curates multimedia artefacts, disseminating them through channels such as websites, webinars, and open source repositories; and finally the networker, who actively triggers interaction via social media applications and online learning communities. Additionally, the final chapters offer a blueprint for the future digital scholar as a professional learner and as a "change agent" who is open to and actively pursues innovation.

This book is a guide for those willing to enhance their digital academic profile. It equips a broad readership with the skills and the mindset to harness new digital developments and navigate the ever-evolving digital age. It gives them some fundamentals to build upon, some pointers and indicators to move forward, and some critical insights to reflect on. In other words, this handbook gives the readers answers to how they can evolve as digital scholars.

The emphasis of the book will be on higher education, and most of the book will concentrate on the specific academic context. Nevertheless, we argue that many more people could recognise themselves in what we present. We think of people involved in all kinds of teaching (like academic developers, trainers, instructors, coaches); people working in research institutions; those interested in thinking about their own work in terms of action research; or people with a mission in the (digital) society of today. Although our examples and good practices will mainly come from the academic world, we hope to inspire and get inspired by digital scholars outside academia.

This book aims to be a handbook, i.e., in between a purely scientific and a merely popularising book. We describe the scientific basis, of course, in the style of a decent academic publication, but we do not overload the book with typical research-oriented references and footnotes. We hope you can appreciate our efforts to balance between a truly academic and a more informal, colloquial approach. When we sometimes tend to lean a little more to one side, that simply reflects how we live and work as individual digital scholars in diverse settings, flexible enough to adapt quickly and always professional to practise what we preach. We therefore start from our personal experiences in our own academic lives. We try to explain and illustrate the topics in a practical way so that a large variety of readers with different backgrounds and levels of knowledge find them interesting and handy, full of inspiring insights and examples to apply into their own practice and evolvement as digital scholars. And by the way: isn't 'a digital scholar' someone who intrinsically mixes theory (scholar) and practice (digital)? Think about it!

How to read this book?

In the first chapter of the book a framework will be offered that describes an evolving digital scholar along three dimensions, one of which is chosen to structure the rest of the book. Indeed, we will tackle the different roles a digital scholar can play one by one and devote a separate chapter to each of them. It would be a good idea to read these chapters in the same order as they are presented in the book. Such a linear walkthrough lets the reader/practitioner gradually evolve as digital scholar: it does not only give the reader an insight into the different roles he or she can take on, but it also clarifies how these roles differ and are building upon each other at the same time, relating them to the overall framework.

On the other hand, for the more advanced or, should we say, the more adventurous reader, it is also perfectly possible to choose the chapter of your interest and start from there. As said, the authors worked in a team, but wrote their chapters independently and therefore the chapters have a stand-alone character as well. So, if you are an experienced digital scholar wanting to evolve further, or if you simply want to reread some parts, or if you just want to browse freely through the contents of this book, you can. We help the reader to make a proper selection of a chapter to read by listing briefly what will be tackled at the beginning of each chapter. In this case it is however recommended to start with the first chapter at least, in order to have the framework in mind when later jumping around through the rest of the book.

And for all readers, we invite you to become our critical friends. It is a characteristic of an evolving digital scholar that you constantly reflect upon your own behaviour in the digital world, and that implies that you are critical about what you see, hear, feel, learn and… read. We welcome all constructive comments to improve this book and yes, we intend to update it whenever the time calls for it. New versions (especially of the e-book) will become readily available as soon as there is a need. Please, always check whether you are reading the most recent version.

To all evolving digital scholars, happy reading and practising!

1

The Digital Scholar Framework

Wim Van Petegem

In this chapter we focus on

- ✓ A description of digital technologies and how they shaped the digital world of today in general.
- ✓ The need to develop digital competences for everyone and especially for scholars.
- ✓ Different existing frameworks to name, define and structure needed digital competences.
- ✓ The development of a three-dimensional Digital Scholar Framework that underpins the rest of this book.

Keywords: Digital technologies; digital world; digital competences; digital scholar framework.

1.1   The Digital World

It goes beyond saying that the world in which we are living nowadays is different from the one we lived in some decades ago, even some years ago. Our world (both our planet and our environment) is changing dramatically and quickly. Technology, and in particular information and communication technology (ICT), is one of the driving forces for these innovations, for good and sometimes for bad. For younger people it is hard to imagine a world in which there were no computers, no internet, no Wi-Fi, no social media. And for us, it is impossible to fancy which new electronic devices and digital applications will determine our future lives. Yet, we must cope with this new world, its opportunities and its challenges. Therefore, it is important we understand where we come from and where we are heading to in this digital world.

We don't want to teach computer history here – there are better resources for this. However, we cannot deny that one of the major breakthroughs in the digitisation of the world was the introduction of the personal computer somewhere in the 80s. We moved from gigantic mainframes with far-end terminals to desktop computers, bringing computing power within reach. Several generations of microprocessors and improved display technologies have ultimately resulted in smaller and handier devices, like laptops and tablets. This evolution was accompanied by a similar transformation in telecommunication, from plain old telephone services (the so-called POTS, for those who still remember this acronym) to mobile telephony with a whole set of intermediate technologies. Needless to say, the smartphone as we know it today can be seen as a fusion between the two: we can still call but we can do so many more things with this device comparable to what we used to do with our computer.

Another milestone in this history is the development of the Internet and the worldwide web at the beginning of the 90s. Gradually, the world became more and more connected, literally with cables above and under the ground and even under the sea. This entire infrastructure has already been renewed a few times, with ever more efficient technologies, in that we no longer need the cables to connect our (personal) devices. More so, we expect that we will be connected with these devices anywhere, anytime, with sufficient bandwidth in order to e.g., watch television while commuting by train back home from work. The latter example hides another evolution, namely with the browser technology. Initially it was developed to hyperlink plain text documents, but it nowadays includes real-time streaming of high-definition multimedia contents. Another related aspect is the rise of social media. People wanted not only to retrieve information but also to contribute and share their own material with their family, friends, peers, community and, why not, the whole world. This gave a totally new dimension to 'being connected', from pure physically plugging in your device to virtually linking online with your own network of acquaintances. It also implies a much broader geographical perspective on your own world. Until not so long ago our view was primarily oriented towards the immediate local environment, but thanks to the potential of ICT we have now a more global outlook. However, there are voices that caution that we may have exaggerated a little in that respect and that we should go 'glocal' where we focus on the integration of the best of both worlds.

The above transformations in technology were accompanied by similar changes in our societal environment. It is commonly accepted that the introduction of ICT has pushed us from the industrial society into the information society. That is a society in which information is considered as a valuable resource, that citizens can create, use, share, manipulate, integrate, etc. to the benefit of their economic, political, cultural or other activities. One step further was the creation of a knowledge society which transformed information into added value, resources or actual knowledge that allows the members of the society to improve their human condition and living standards. Nowadays, the concept of a network society describes the world in which we are living pretty well. According to Manuel Castells (2010), a network society is a society where its structures, organisations and activities are substantially based and relying on (digital) information and communication networks. One could wonder what would be the next step: will it be the wisdom society as described by Dalal (2008)?

What we know for sure, is the fact that ICT has led to applications and innovations in all sectors of economic activity: health care (telemedicine, robot surgery, electronic health records, etc.), finances (e-banking, cashless payments, cryptocurrencies, etc.), commerce (e-invoices, online shopping, etc.), tourism (online travel agencies, e-hospitality, etc.), transport (navigation systems, self-driving cars, etc.), culture (virtual museums, internet radio and television, etc.), government (e-ID, electronic voting, tele-administration, etc.), and others. New, sometimes disruptive business models are necessary to implement these innovations, and therefore need to be invented, always taking into account their advantages and disadvantages. Issues like accessibility, trust, cost, accountability, transparency, convenience, speed, acceptance should be paid proper attention to. And yes, also education does not escape from this tendency, but that will be explained in more detail later in this book.

Next to, or maybe even due to, the technological changes, people have changed as well. We might have heard of the Baby Boomers, typically born in the two decades after the Second World War. They are preceding Generation X, the cohort born from the early-to-mid 1960s to the early 1980s. This generation was followed by the Millennials, also known as Generation Y, with birth years between the early 1980s and the mid-1990s to early 2000s. This is the first generation of young people coming of age in the information society, and as a result they learnt very easily to use digital technologies and social media. The current demographic cohort is called Generation Z. These youngsters were born in a world full of technology and have used ICT tools and in particular the internet from early childhood on. They can simply not imagine a world without and expect ubiquitous access to the internet, with ever smaller devices and at a low, preferably no cost. And these young people are entering higher education now.

All the above evolutions indicate that the world in which we are living, working and learning has changed a lot thanks to, or at least due to, the technological changes. The adoption of ICT in our daily lives has a tremendous impact on all our activities. It is difficult to predict where this is going to in the long run, but even in the short term, we can hardly foresee which innovations new digital technologies might bring. And it is in this digital world that a Digital Scholar must survive. Before we start with the survival trip, we need to make sure we are talking a common language, i.e., we need to define what we mean by 'digital technologies', 'digital competences' and a 'Digital Scholar', all in the context of higher education.

1.2 Digital Technologies

The word 'digital' comes from the Latin word 'digitus' (finger), by the way one of the oldest tools used for counting. And the word 'technology' stems from the Greek word 'tekhnē' (art, craft) and 'logia' denoting a subject of study or interest.

The combination of words 'digital technology' started to be used in the middle of last century, when engineers built the first computing system, using the theory developed by the 17th-century German mathematician, Gottfried Wilhelm Leibniz. His concept was based on a binary code, consisting of 0s and 1s (called bits), rather than the decimal numeral system we are more familiar with. The first (non-mechanical) calculating system was comprised of vacuum tubes to implement this binary code. But soon, with the introduction of the semiconductor transistor, this technology could be miniaturised dramatically. This in turn allowed one to compress huge (at the time) amounts of bits in a small device, where they could be stored, transformed, retrieved and transmitted in an easy way. And that was the major breakthrough for digital technology. Where the early computers were merely seen as number crunchers, i.e., manipulating large sets of data in a rather simple way, the technology became more and more sophisticated and allowed more and more complex processes. Until today new technologies are emerging and adding to this evolution: internet of things, artificial intelligence, blockchain technology, augmented reality, etc.

While in the beginning the term 'digital technology' was mainly describing a computing device, i.e., a tangible piece of equipment, nowadays the term is used with a much broader meaning. It could include not only devices but also digital platforms, systems, tools and apps, infrastructure, processes, services, methods, resources, and so on. A taxonomy to bring some order to this apparently chaotic multitude of digital technologies could help but is hard to find, although some attempts have been made by, for instance, Berger (2018). For the purpose of this book, it is sufficient to realise that there is a wide spectrum of digital technologies available to users.

It is more important to recognise what is called the affordance of the digital technology at stake. An affordance is "the quality or property of an object that defines its possible uses or makes clear how it can or should be used".[3] In the literature there is some discussion whether this refers to an inherent characteristic of the object, rather than a property which is attributed by the environment or context. Alternatively, is it perceived by the user of the object, i.e., is affordance related to utility (usefulness) or to usability? Both meanings have their value and could be used in this book. Matt Bower (2008, pp.6-7) classifies the affordances of digital technologies in the context of higher education as follows in terms of 'abilities':

1. Media affordances – the type of input and output forms, such as text ("read-ability", "write-ability"), images ("view-ability", "draw-ability"), audio ("listen-ability", "speak-ability"), video ("watch-ability", "video-produce-ability").

2. Spatial affordances – the ability to resize elements within an interface ("resize-ability"), move and place elements within an interface ("move-ability").

3. Temporal affordances – access anytime anywhere (accessibility), ability to be recorded ("record-ability") and played back ("playback-ability"), synchronous versus asynchronous ("synchronicity").

4. Navigation affordances – capacity to browse to other sections of a resource and move back/forward ("browse-ability"), capacity to link to other sections within the resource or other resources ("link-ability"), ability to search ("search-ability") and sort and sequence ("data-manipulation-ability").

5. Emphasis affordances – capacity to highlight aspects of a resources ("highlight-ability"), explicitly direct attention to particular components ("focus-ability").

6. Synthesis affordances – capacity to combine multiple tools together to create a mixed media learning environment ("combine-ability"), the extent to which the functions of tools and the content of resources can be integrated ("integrate-ability").

7. Access-control affordances – capacity to allow or deny who can read/edit/upload/down-load/broadcast/view/administer ("permission-ability"), capacity to support one–one/one–many/many–many contributions and collaborations ("share-ability").

8. Technical affordances – capacity to be used on various platforms with minimal/ubiquitous underlying technologies, ability to adapt to bandwidth of connection, speed & efficiency of tool/s.

9. Usability – intuitiveness of tool, ease with which user can manipulate tool to execute its various functions, relates to efficiency.

10. Aesthetics – appeal of design, appearance of interface, relates to user satisfaction and ability to hold attention.
11. Reliability – robustness of platform, system performs as intended whenever required.

Although the list dates from 2008, Bower and colleagues (2015) have continued their work and expanded the list by, for example, including wearable devices. Understanding and appreciating affordances of digital tools come in handy when a Digital Scholar will have to assess the potential of a certain digital technology for his or her academic work.

One final note here is on the adjective 'digital'. One can argue whether it is still necessary to use this term: is not all technology nowadays in one or another way digital? Or, put differently, does the digitisation not go so far that it is commonly accepted, and even simply assumed? Hence, the digital aspect becomes a sort of natural characteristic of all technology, and as such it becomes an obsolete distinctive descriptor that might as well be dropped. We already see that many ICT supported activities are becoming more and more generalised, and the technology itself is becoming invisible. As an example, we are getting so used to cashless payments that we no longer realise the whole (digital and technological) infrastructure behind. Some authors, like Paiva et al. (2016), tried to apply this idea of technology becoming ubiquitous and invisible to the world of education as well and they describe we are moving from e-learning back to learning again. For the purpose of this book, we will continue to use the term digital technologies, to make it clear we are not talking about other forms of technology such as books, etc.

1.3   Digital Competences

The advance of all these digital technologies requires new skills from their users which implies that they need to have digital competences. What does that mean?

It is widely accepted that 'competence' could be defined as one's ability to mobilise knowledge, skills, attitude, insights and values in order to perform a given task successfully in a certain context. In the world of today, our contexts have become more and more digital with tasks also being performed by digital technologies. So, 'digital competence' could be simply defined as 'the competence to act in today's digital world'. What that entails, will be explained below.

Limited research articles are published on this topic, but we could find some policy documents that, for example, were published by the European Commission. The commission developed a Digital Competence Framework for all European citizens, version 2.0, in 2016.[4] This framework identifies the key components of digital competence in 5 areas which can be summarised as below:

1. Information and data literacy:
   - ✓ To articulate information needs, to locate and retrieve digital data, information and content.
   - ✓ To judge the relevance of the source and its content.
   - ✓ To store, manage, and organise digital data, information and content.
2. Communication and collaboration:
   - ✓ To interact, communicate and collaborate through digital technologies while being aware of cultural and generational diversity.
   - ✓ To participate in society through public and private digital services and participatory citizenship.
   - ✓ To manage one's digital identity and reputation.
3. Digital content creation:
   - ✓ To create and edit digital content.
   - ✓ To improve and integrate information and content into an existing body of knowledge while understanding how copyright and licences are to be applied.
   - ✓ To know how to give understandable instructions for a computer system.
4. Safety:
   - ✓ To protect devices, content, personal data and privacy in digital environments.
   - ✓ To protect physical and psychological health, and to be aware of digital technologies for social well-being and social inclusion.
   - ✓ To be aware of the environmental impact of digital technologies and their use.
5. Problem solving:
   - ✓ To identify needs and problems, and to resolve conceptual problems and problem situations in digital environments.
   - ✓ To use digital tools to innovate processes and products.
   - ✓ To keep up to date with the digital evolution.

The commission also developed a specific framework for educators, called DigCompEdu.[5]

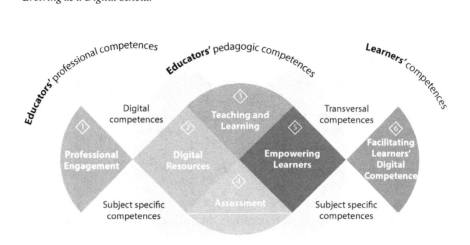

Figure 1.1: Digital Competence Framework for Educators (© European Union, 1995-2021, licensed under CC BY 4.0)

This framework provides a general reference frame to support the development of educator-specific digital competences in Europe, at all levels of education. DigCompEdu details 22 sub-competences organised into six areas:

- ✓ Area 1 focuses on the professional environment;
- ✓ Area 2 on sourcing, creating and sharing digital resources;
- ✓ Area 3 on managing and orchestrating the use of digital tools in teaching and learning;
- ✓ Area 4 on digital tools and strategies to enhance assessment;
- ✓ Area 5 on the use of digital tools to empower learners;
- ✓ Area 6 on facilitating learners' digital competence.

Areas 2 to 5 form the pedagogic core of the framework. They detail the competences educators need to possess to foster effective, inclusive and innovative learning strategies, using digital technologies.

Another valuable resource is the work done by JISC,[6] the UK higher, further education and skills sectors' not-for-profit organisation for digital services and solutions. JISC talks about 'digital capabilities' as opposed to digital competences. At the individual level they define a framework for digital capabilities with the following six elements:

- ✓ ICT Proficiency (functional skills)
- ✓ Information, data and media literacies (critical use)

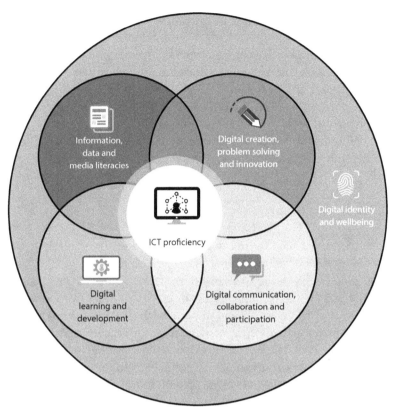

Figure 1.2: Building digital capabilities: the six elements defined (based on the figure by JISC, licensed under CC BY-NC-SA)

- ✓ Digital creation, problem solving and innovation (creative production)
- ✓ Digital communication, collaboration and partnership (participation)
- ✓ Digital learning and development (development)
- ✓ Digital identity and wellbeing (self-actualising)

Interestingly JISC presents this framework not only for staff and students, but it also refers to digital capabilities at the organisational level. We indeed need to look beyond the capabilities of individuals and consider the extent to which the culture and infrastructure of an institution enable and motivate digital practices, but this is beyond the scope of this book.

The above frameworks are creditable attempts to describe the complexity of digital competences by breaking them down into more recognisable components and ordering these in a meaningful way. These frameworks are valuable in order to understand what is expected from us, individuals, citizens, teachers, scholars, living and working in a digital world. They often come together with instruments to measure to what extent or to what level one has reached (partial aspects of) digital competence. And moreover, they offer some pointers on how to become more digitally proficient, i.e., on how to move from one level to the next one on the digital competence ladder. We will not elaborate further on these frameworks here, but we invite the reader to go and study the indicated references if interested in more details.

1.4   The Digital Scholar

Scholars are people who devote themselves to study, particularly to an area in which they have developed expertise.[7] For a more extensive description of a scholar please refer to the work of Boyer (1990). The traditional concept of scholarship was viewed as the scientific discovery of new knowledge and had been the centre of academic life and was crucial to an institution's advancement for decades. Boyer articulated a new paradigm for faculty scholarly activity, because it needed to be broadened and made more flexible to include not only the new social and environmental challenges beyond the campus but also the reality of contemporary life. He came up with four functions of scholarship:

- ✓ The Scholarship of Discovery – This focuses on the creation of new knowledge in a specific area or discipline, and is thus often taken to be synonymous with research.
- ✓ The Scholarship of Integration – This aspect emphasises the synthesis of (new) knowledge by linking topics within one discipline, or by making connections across disciplines. It requires the placement of specialities in larger contexts by illuminating data in a revealing way that makes them accessible and educating non-specialists.
- ✓ The Scholarship of Application (later also called the Scholarship of Engagement) – This function relates to the concept of service within or outside the university, which might include peer-reviewing journal articles or grant applications and sitting on various committees. It also includes, for instance, input into policy making and general media discussions.
- ✓ The Scholarship of Teaching – This aspect is more than just focusing on teaching – it includes the systematic self-study combined with peer review of our own practice of teaching. By emphasising this aspect, an attempt is made to raise the profile of teaching.

Each of the three traditional forms of scholarship (teaching, research, and community service) can be seen to perform all four functions of scholarship as defined by Boyer (discovery, integration, application, and teaching).

Who then, is the Digital Scholar? Again, we could simply say that this is a scholar living and working in the digital age. Weller (2018) defines a digital scholar as someone who employs digital, networked and open approaches to demonstrate specialism in a certain disciplinary field. The 'digital' and to some extent also the 'networked' component in this definition have been addressed above, but we will come back to this and the 'open approaches' later in the book.

Traditionally we think of a scholar as a recognised academic, a person who works as a teacher or researcher at a university or other higher education institution, and who usually holds an advanced degree. For this book we do not necessarily look at academic staff (faculty), but e.g., professional and support staff in teaching and learning centres or educational consultants without any institutional affiliation could also qualify as scholars, and especially as digital scholars. Everyone scholarly active (according to the above-mentioned functions of modern scholarship) in a digital, networked, open world could call themselves a digital scholar.

1.5 The Digital Scholar Framework

In order further to analyse the concept of digital scholarship, we present our own digital scholar framework and its key components which we will be using throughout the book as our golden thread.

We consider three distinct 'dimensions' in the concept of a digital scholar.

1.5.1 *The Digital Scholar as a Human Being*

First of all, a digital scholar is an individual human being. This means that s/he has a certain, unique personality that comprises his/her identity, including a digital identity. S/he is fully aware of her/himself and is taking an own stance, an own position in the digital world, as a single person. Nevertheless, this always happens in relation to others. A digital scholar is member of a team with like-minded colleagues in the own discipline, the own department or any similar entity, using amongst others digital technologies to bond together. The teams themselves belong to a bigger organisation, usually the institution (i.e., university or any other higher education institution). Digital scholars are employees of this institution, which entitles them to work across various borders, such as interfaculty or interdisciplinary. The

Figure 1.3: The Digital Scholar Framework, as developed by the authors

academic institution, usually comprising one or multiple physical campuses, or maybe a virtual one, is no longer an ivory tower. It is embedded in a local community, a society of which the digital scholar is an active participant, in two ways: digital scholars bring back their knowledge and expertise into the society and vice versa is society triggering the work and expertise building of the digital scholar. Finally, a digital scholar is also a global citizen. It has already been said that thanks to the digital technologies the world has become more open and more connected, enabling digital scholars to collaborate with peers across the globe, and to share their expertise with virtually the whole world.

This dimension is represented in the figure by concentric circles, symbolising the fact that it all starts from yourself, and in the ever-growing action radius of the environment in which a digital scholar is operating.

1.5.2 *The Digital Scholar as an Academic*

By far the most obvious dimension in the framework is dealing with what we need to do. In other words, what we are supposed to do as academics, as scholars in our daily encounters. A digital scholar works in an academic environment where s/he is involved in research, teaching and service. The latter is sometimes also referred to as community service, social impact, science communication and/or outreach. For the purpose of this book, we will be referring to the traditional triad of academic life and not Boyer's forms of scholarship.

This dimension is represented by moving arrows which implies that these activities are always there in the back of our minds. The arrows also suggest that all three types of activities follow each other but at the same time inspire each other as well. It must be clear that a digital scholar, like any other scholar, is always balancing between these three aspects, and sometimes even jumping from one to the other, not necessarily in the order as indicated in the framework. Typical for a digital scholar is that s/he is able to benefit from the advantages that digital technologies offer for academic work, for the three aspects separately, but also and maybe above all, for an integrated approach to these three aspects.

1.5.3 *The Digital Scholar as a Role Player*

Maybe the most challenging dimension in the framework is the one related to different roles a digital scholar could play. With this aspect we want to emphasise that a digital scholar is not just a human being, is not just doing what is expected from someone in an academic environment, but s/he actively takes up a role in the digital world of today. Digital scholars use their (digital) competences at different levels, and that could potentially lead to different roles they play. We distinguish five of them for the purpose of this book, from simply using words (as an 'author'), over bringing a strong message (as a 'storyteller') and illustrating the story with media (as a 'creator'), to packaging the message with all media included (as an 'integrator') and ultimately sharing it with a larger audience (as a 'networker'). This will be the core of the book and each of these roles will be explained in full detail in the next chapters.

These roles are presented in the framework as a pie chart. It could be argued that there is a sort of hierarchy in the different roles, based on the level of digital competences needed to play the specific role. The role of 'author' would then be the easiest, simple role, with only a basic set of digital competences, while a 'networker' would have the richest set of these competences. We are not denying that there is some truth in this view, and actually

29

we will use this logical order as guideline for the book. Nevertheless, we would like to emphasise that in reality a digital scholar feels comfortable in constantly switching between the roles and maybe even taking up multiple roles at once, depending on the occasion. Of course, this demands a high level of digital competences.

1.6   Evolving as a Digital Scholar

Indeed, the whole idea of the Digital Scholar framework is to move within and between the three specified dimensions of a digital scholar as a human being, as an academic, and as a role player. It is tempting inherently to interpret some of the dimensional aspects in terms of levels of maturity. And to a certain extent this is true. However, evolving as a digital scholar not only refers to linearly growing and developing digital competences, but also to exploring, hopping around and jumping back and forth, sometimes failing, sometimes succeeding, but always and steadily acquiring new competences in a more complex, sophisticated way.

The European Commission uses the metaphor of learning to swim when it comes to developing digital competences[8] in relation to its Digital Competence framework. As swimming is a skill we all have to learn, this metaphor very well fits for developing as a digital scholar as well. In the beginning you only dare to put your toes into the cold water. After exercising the swimming movements on dry land, you carefully enter the water, the shallow water of course, and with the help of the trainer (and maybe a swim ring) you splash around a bit until you can also perform the practised movements in the water without any help. Once you have got there, you start to enjoy it, and you venture in the deeper water as well. Sometimes it is hard to keep your head above water, though you feel safe as there will always be a lifeguard around in the swimming pool. For the more adventurous amongst us, a next step is to swim in the wild water, in the sea (or even the ocean, as the European Commission suggests). Or, if you prefer, you start with deep diving. And why not, you can also become an instructor, or a lifeguard yourself. Ample opportunities to become more experienced, and to share your expertise with others.

It must be clear that also as a digital scholar we will first have to set a few small steps, then to practise a lot before we eventually enjoy and can take on new roles.

1.7   How to understand and use the Digital Scholar framework

As indicated, in this book we will focus on the dimension of the framework that refers to the different roles a digital scholar can play. The chapters are organised accordingly. We aim to deepen and broaden these roles by explaining what they entail, but also what kind of digital competences are considered as vital in this role. Each role will also be linked with the other two dimensions of the framework. Indeed, while playing a role, a digital scholar should not forget he or she is a human being as well as an academic. Moreover, the development of digital competences should not be limited to the 'roles' part, but should be seen in a more integrated way, including the two other dimensions too. It is not our aim to each time make a full coverage of all elements in the framework, though we hope to give enough background, good practices and inspiring examples for the future digital scholar to fill in the blanks or connect the dots according to own insights.

We already mentioned that a digital scholar is not constrained in one role, nor in one aspect of the two other dimensions. In other words, a digital scholar cannot be caught in just one cell of the framework or should not go through the framework in a simple linear way. A digital scholar should be agile or flexible enough to jump around, to find the right balance and maybe to combine different aspects together in the daily practice. When reading the book, the framework should be seen as something dynamic, a spinning wheel or a rolling ball, with stretchy and sometimes moving boundaries. Being able to cross the imaginary borders between the cells in the framework is an essential capability of a digital scholar.

We hope to take you on a journey with this framework and provide you with a trustful compass to find your way, to evolve and become a digital scholar in action!

References

Berger, S., Denner, M.-S., & Roeglinger, M. (2018). The Nature of Digital Technologies – Development of a Multi-Layer Taxonomy. *Research papers 92*. Retrieved from https://aisel.aisnet.org/ecis2018_rp/92.

Bower, M. (2008). Affordance analysis – matching learning tasks with learning technologies. *Educational Media International*, 45(1), 3–15. https://doi.org/10.1080/09523980701847115

Bower, M. & Sturman D. (2015) What are the educational affordances of wearable technologies? *Computers & Education*, Volume 88, Pages 343-353, ISSN 0360-1315, https://doi.org/10.1016/j.compedu.2015.07.013.

Boyer, E.L. (1990) *Scholarship reconsidered: Priorities of the professoriate*. Princeton, New Jersey: Princeton University Press, The Carnegie Foundation for the Advancement of Teaching.

Castells, M. (2010) *The Rise of the Network Society*. West Sussex: Blackwell Publishing.

Dalal, N. (2008) Wisdom Networks: Towards a Wisdom-Based Society. In: Lytras M.D. et al. (eds) *The Open Knowledge Society. A Computer Science and Information Systems Manifesto*. WSKS 2008. *Communications in Computer and Information Science*, vol 19. Springer, Berlin, Heidelberg. https://doi.org/10.1007/978-3-540-87783-7_2.

Paiva, J., Morais, C., Costa, L., & Pinheiro, A. (2016). The shift from "e-learning" to "learning": Invisible technology and the dropping of the "e." *British Journal of Educational Technology*, 47(2), 226–238. https://doi.org/10.1111/bjet.12242

Weller, M. (2018). *The Digital Scholar. How Technology is Transforming Scholarly Practice*. In The Digital Scholar: Philosopher's Lab (Vol. 1). https://doi.org/10.5840/dspl2018111

2
The Digital Scholar as Author:
Choices in disseminating scholarly work

Sonja Strydom

In this chapter we focus on

✓ An overview of the changing educational arena of scholarly authorship.
✓ The different paths digital scholars can consider to disseminate knowledge.
✓ The evolution from paper-based practices to open access digital platforms.
✓ A basic theoretical understanding of choices made by digital scholars.
✓ Approaches that could be considered in raising awareness of our scholarly beliefs.

Keywords: Authorship; digital scholar; academic identity; social media; open access publishing.

2.1   Introduction

Authors write and create with a particular audience in mind. In the case of higher education research, the focus is usually on the academic and professional support community. Feedback on our scholarly opinions is traditionally rooted in conference feedback, peer reviews or critical friends. Such views call for us to engage critically with our own voice and how it potentially impacts the broader community – either at a micro level (ourselves, team, institutionally), mesa level (society), or macro level (globally).

The advances in digital technologies provide more opportunity for the assimilation of various research communities than ever before. These continuously evolving platforms pave the way for "new knowledge ecologies" and "three ages of the journal" as scholars realign themselves from text to digital and multimedia interaction (Peters et al., 2016, p. 1402). However, these approaches chosen by an increasing number of scholars require essential reconsiderations of the use of 'digital text' in an open access world of academe. As can be expected, these disruptions have profound impact on the conventional practices associated with journal-based knowledge, the traditional formats of altmetric and the current peer-review systems globally in place (Peters et al., 2016).

This chapter suggests a critical rethink of conventional scholarly practices to include various forms of digital scholarship. Essentially, the majority of academic scholars are already embroiled in some level of 'digital' through means of our teaching and learning (T&L) practices. For example, during the lecture via the use of PowerPoint or the institution's online learning management system, at a social level in terms of social media and other associated approaches and tools, or then the submission of scholarly papers via digital systems. Despite these common practices, an alternative engagement with digital scholarship could provide opportunity to critically rethink the format of how knowledge could be disseminated, how scientific knowledge will be translated to a broader audience and how to engage with such an audience.

Digital scholarship does not necessarily require someone to be an academic, yet it also does not suggest that anyone who use digital platforms for knowledge dissemination are digital scholars. This chapter argues that a digital scholar is viewed as someone who "employs digital, networked and open approaches to demonstrate specialism in a field" (Weller, 2018, p. 8). It is with this explanation in mind that the next section explores the role of academic authorship, and how it aligns with our digital identities.

Providing us with some essential theoretical underpinnings, this chapter aims to provide the reader with a meta-level understanding of why we have certain preferences in our teaching and learning, research and community involvement practices and the manner in which we choose to disseminate our scholarly work.

2.2   Academic authorship and its relation to the disciplinary field and online

Scholarly authorship represents the core business of higher education – namely the creation and dissemination of knowledge. Academics as authors are expected to continually "read, analyse, assess and compare written texts, such as reports, academic papers and books, undergraduate assignments, postgraduate dissertations and doctorates. They also produce written teaching materials and textbooks for student consumption along with research reports, monographs, articles and textbooks for publication" (French, 2019, p. 3). These practices remain critical in the daily operations of academic scholars but are becoming increasingly complex with the rise of digital technologies in education.

The rapid development of digital technologies in all spheres of life has a significant impact on the manner in which scholars can communicate with each other and a broader community (Zou & Hyland, 2019). Authorship within the digitised world has evolved from the conventional printed version of research papers to digital publishing, online-only publications (peer-reviewed), academic social media platforms and other non-conventional methods of sharing our scholarly voice by means of video and/or audio recordings and academic blogs.

Consequently, academic authorship is becoming increasingly multifaceted and is often characterised by authors competing to be noticed for their scholarly work (Laakso, Lindman, Shen, Nyman, & Björk, 2017). These trends are not unexpected since there are currently more than 28 000 active journals alone that publish more than 2.5 million academic papers annually. It is this 'overcrowding' and increasing complexities that inspire many researchers to call for alternative ways in which digital technologies could assist (through, for example, open peer review and open access) in the challenges associated with sharing the scholarly voice (Laakso et al., 2017).

2.1.1 *The impact of field, capital and habitus on digital scholarship*
In order to fully understand the different reasons and approaches scholars consider when sharing their scientific work, it is important to recognise the influence of the different disciplinary fields, what is valued within such field and also the dispositions of authors.

The relational field approach can explain many of our authorial deliberations. Bourdieu argues that the social world comprises various independent fields. These autonomous fields are depicted by their own systems and rationality and may be influenced by the changing nature of other fields they are associated with (Shammas & Sandberg, 2015). For example, if an author specialises in the field of higher education, trends and influences in the field of educational technology could potentially influence the former. These different intersecting fields emerge as 'sub-spaces' that emphasise particular activities and are governed by their own rules and agreements (Hilgers & Mangez, 2015).

Within these disciplinary fields, agents and structures (e.g., scholars and institutions) are continuously in competition in terms of access to resources and position that provide them with the necessary 'currency' to dictate and influence the fields they operate in (Shammas & Sandberg, 2015). Consequently, these various role players in the different fields (e.g., individuals, groups or institutions) strive continuously to increase their standing. The actions and choices of these role players are influenced by the underlying structuring principles of their respective fields (Maton, 2005).

For example, in the case of higher education, research and its impact will provide scholars with particular status and standing in the fields they operate in. As the different fields evolve in autonomy, the likelihood increases that they generate scholars who are known for particular competence and expertise (Hilgers & Mangez, 2015). It becomes a space wherein scholars and the different groups they represent are positioned (Vandenberghe, 2017).

As mentioned earlier, we as scholars could be associated with more than one field and/or community which could cause tensions in the expectations situated within such communities. Inevitably, these differing expectations are aligned with our scholarly identity and how we identify ourselves within such a community (Nygaard, 2017). For instance, we may feel associated with a particular institutional perspective or field such as HE, but also experience a close alignment with our own disciplinary background, different intersecting fields that resonate with our own research interests and so forth (Nygaard, 2017). Attempting to negotiate and accommodate these opposing expectations could result in authors entering what are called 'sites of negotiation' (p. 520) where we deal with conflicting calls – whether personally or externally – that could impact our choices in the processes of forming or disseminating scholarly findings (Nygaard, 2017).

Bourdieu's field theory stresses fields as potential "arenas of force and arenas of struggle" (Ferrare & Apple, 2015, p. 48). We as scholars can experience fields either as opportunities to display our influence, but similarly, also as an arena of strain. With reference to the former, fields could constitute spaces of normative rules and values where those that agree with such rules and values agree with such rules or values are compensated. These expectations and rules within fields are, however, often challenged, which results in these fields becoming areas of struggle (Ferrare & Apple, 2015).

What we struggle for in fields is recognition and access to what is called capital – in other words – what is being valued within a particular field (Hilgers & Mangez, 2015). The perceived 'capital' associated with, for instance, scientific high impact peer reviewed journal papers that directly influence career prospects still dictates many scholars' choices in knowledge dissemination. Often it results in the inability of alternative scholarly authorial approaches to compete with the more conventional approaches to authorship. The status of journals, choice of types of publications, the impact and acknowledgement of our scholarly expertise all influence our choices in where and how to publish our work. It is therefore important that we as digital scholars recognise the 'capital' in our respective fields and how it will influence our choices in terms of digital scholarship. Are we restricted in our methods due to a more conventional approach to publication and scholarship, or are our fields (and peers) providing us with the flexibility to explore and experiment with alternative methodologies in demonstrating our knowledge and skills?

To conclude, another aspect that impacts our choices is what is called habitus. Habitus, as highlighted by Bourdieu, relates to often unconscious dispositions of scholars, and the way these dispositions influence the choices that we make within the field. It refers to our responses under specific circumstances and situations. In a sense, habitus reflects our pasts, but it also impacts the future and impending choices we make (English & Bolton, 2016). We will often take a particular position in a field based on the influence of habitus (Ferrare & Apple, 2015).

It is then against this background with the different undertows in fields, the perceived capital associated with the workings within the fields we operate in, as well as the impact of habitus, that we make choices in publicising our scientific work.

2.1.2 *Academic identity in a digitised world*

One of the main issues that academics are confronted with in the digital educational context is the aspect of openness. Traditionally, before the rapid growth of the internet, we were fairly 'protected' or 'safe' due to the regulations placed on scholarly writing. For instance, conventional journal publications follow a robust peer-review system which inevitably equates to a prolonged time before scientific work is published. Access to such journals in the past was also limited to a distinct audience of interest. In recent times, however, the digital world has provided the opportunity for scholars to build ever-growing networks and receive feedback from individuals unknown to themselves.

We can argue that scholarly writing could be positioned as part of identity development within an educational context. It implies that we are continuously in the process of portraying ourselves professionally through, amongst other things, our scholarly writing (French, 2019). Based on the different fields we represent, the different levels of involvement within such fields and the manner in which these fields are constructed, all impact the ever-evolving nature of our scholarly identity (French, 2019).

However, to make meaning of scholarly identity it is necessary to develop a grasp of the deeper bases of specifically online (digital) identity. By exploring our 'world views' (i.e., the way in which we believe the world functions) in terms of our own identity will enable others to appreciate our willingness and often unwillingness to engage with online practices (Hildebrandt & Couros, 2016). In many instances, for example, we choose to share only certain aspects of our identity with a broader (perhaps unforgiving) public audience as opposed to a more intimate, safe community of colleagues where relations have been built over years. However, we are increasingly obliged to consider online platforms as modes of sharing new knowledge due to "[it becoming] both impractical and disadvantageous as institutions, and society in general, [that] become enmeshed with digital practice and culture" (Hildebrandt & Couros, 2016, p. 89). We then have to negotiate our options and also our own intrinsic values and aspirations in terms of our own intellectual standing in the fields we represent. This is of particular relevance to our own public reputation.

The complexities associated with the development of an online identity do have implications for our consideration of the modes by which we create and share knowledge. For instance, if the argument is made that identity is precise and not fluid, it implies that our online identity should mirror our 'offline' identity. Such an approach inadvertently leads to the sharing of the 'good and the bad' in an online space which could be unforgiving and will always have a record. These practices become even more complex if we choose to engage in online spaces with controversial topics or with critical perspectives that are not necessarily appreciated by such a broader audience.

As we've seen from above, the use of digital technologies in communicating scientific findings therefore starts to blur the boundaries between an academic and a generalist audience. This requires authors/scholars to reconsider our approaches in communicating our findings to a broader audience of interest (Zou & Hyland, 2019). One of the main issues we grapple with is the development of a digital footprint which becomes increasingly complicated to manage and maintain within the ever-evolving digitised world. Such a digitised world is often unwilling to forgive any 'mistakes' with fast judgements made (Hildebrandt & Couros, 2016).

The opportunity for increased visibility in a digital age therefore requires us to consider our publishing strategy and how we are considering crossing the boundary from the conventional publishing approaches to the potentially more 'transformative' digital approaches. The question can rightly be asked whether the use of digital technology resembles the process of boundary crossing from the conventional way in which scholarly authorship is portrayed to a more flexible online mode of scholarly communication. On the other hand, the incorporation of the digital into academic authorship could also potentially accentuate the emergence of a 'boundaryless' evolution from the traditional paper-based and closely scrutinised practices to ones that are more open, democratised and potentially transformational in their being.

2.3 Approaches in conveying scientific ideas to the broader community

With the transformation of the traditional intellectual world into the digital sphere, we are afforded the chance to become consumers and inventors of knowledge on a broader platform. It creates opportunity for a scholarly community based on collaboration and mutual interest which moves beyond the conventional, individualistic approaches to scholarly authorship and knowledge creation.

2.3.1 *Journal Publishing*
One of the ways in which scientific thought is communicated is firmly rooted in the publication of work in reputable journals. In the world of publishing, the growth in new journals provides a wider range of options available that

could contribute to processes of scholarly deliberations. The majority of HE scholars are familiar with the importance of considering the 'traditional' way of publishing in printed form. In many instances scholarly publications in reputable journals still contribute to promotion, tenure and intellectual status within our disciplinary field.

There are a number of factors we take into consideration when choosing a journal for scientific publication. These include the shortlisting of journals representing our field of specialisation; whether there is a robust peer-review system in place and whether it is open access; the history of the journal citation reports, the accreditation of the journal as well as the impact factors associated with a particular journal.

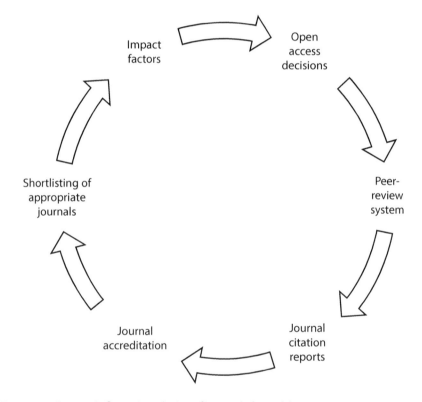

Figure 2.1: Factors influencing choice of journals for publication.

In terms of access, print journals have only mainly be accessible to subscribed users, but with the dawn of digital technologies this landscape changed to a world where academic journals are digitised. Initially this implied that access to such knowledge only evolved to online spaces but, recently, digital technologies transformed and disrupted the conventional landscape of academic authorship and publishing.

Currently, academic publishing via journals consists of three options:
- ✓ Access is granted to an article via a method of payment where the reader becomes responsible for production costs
- ✓ Open access where the author is responsible for production costs
- ✓ Open access where production costs reside with external third parties such as institutions (Peters et al., 2016, p. 1404).

As expected, open access (OA) suggests numerous chances to transform the established modes of publishing knowledge (Peters et al., 2016). Although the open access movement paves the way for "knowledge liberation" it often is crippled by economic or corporate influences such as the impact of large and influential publishing houses (Peters et al., 2016, p. 1406). Typically, scholars are not too enthusiastic about open access journals since these are not usually associated with high impact factors and we receive limited recognition for allowing our publications in open access (Nicholas et al., 2017).

In the consideration of open access publishing, Nicholas et al. (2017) suggest a critical consideration of the following aspects:

Advantages	Disadvantages
Opens the closed world of publication (a reference to firewalls) to more researchers	Tend to be less-established journals that are OA
New ideas can be dispersed more rapidly, widely, and, in turn, this triggers further research	Predatory journals that inhabit the OA space can give a wrong impression of the status of OA journals
Provides more immediate and increased visibility	Quality is low or wholly missing because anyone can publish anything as long as they can pay
Gives more personal control over research work as it can be disseminated more freely	It is not a level playing field; only groups with funding can publish in OA journals and so obtain more citations
Easier to re-use data	Open Archive Repositories do not have embedded peer review systems
Provides a larger audience for a paper	Easier to steal information
Obtain more citations and, hence, an improvement in reputation	Fears of light touch peer review
It is ethical to do so because of the public money involved	It is not a sustainable model, with author publishing fees being so expensive

Table 2.1: A critical reflection of open access publishing.
Source: Nicholas et al. (2017, p. 203).

Conferences are also popular platforms to share our intellectual work on due to the immediate feedback from peers that could ultimately lead to the opportunity to publish work. Conference contributions are differentiated through posters, presentations, publications in conference proceedings and keynotes (Nicholas et al., 2017). The motivation to publish will ultimately guide us in our choices of knowledge dissemination at these types of events. Digital texts, for instance, have an influence on the audience's position and impact the nature of the narrative through providing wider opportunity for clarification and understanding (Peters et al., 2016).

2.3.2 Critical engagement with your scholarly impact (Self, Team, Society, Global)

In the current HE context, it is important to consider strategies to judge the impact of our scholarly work in the broader academic community. In terms of journals, considerations are mainly associated with the impact factors and the h-index of journals (Cabrera, Roy, & Chisolm, 2018). Journal metrics use citation examination to determine the ranking of journals. Different metrics use diverse methodologies but some of the main foundations of journal metrics are rooted in Web of Science, Scopus and Google Scholar metrics.

The increased use of and reference to bibliometrics and rankings can indicate 'quality' of scholarly work due to the status of journals (i.e., the impact factor) as opposed to the true quality of the content itself (Origgi & Ramello, 2015). The IF (impact factor) displays the impact of a particular journal in comparison with others in a particular field. The IF is usually determined by the number of times an article is cited in a calendar year.

There are various strategies we can consider to improve our impact:
- ✓ Use a similar name variation throughout our scholarly career
- ✓ Repetition of keywords in the abstract
- ✓ Allocation of keywords to the paper
- ✓ Submit articles to high impact journals
- ✓ Remember to regularly update our own professional platforms
- ✓ Consider open access that increases the likelihood of drawing attention to our work
- ✓ Try to identify international co-authors for our paper
- ✓ Consider publishing with a team
- ✓ Increase the number of references used in the paper
- ✓ Participate in Wikipedia contributions
- ✓ Use academic blogging to showcase our work
- ✓ Participate in academic networking sites

✓ Make ourselves available for paper reviews
✓ Create a podcast to disseminate our scholarly work
Source: Ebrahim et al. (2013, p.94)

The exponential growth of digital publication, social media and other associated digital formats and platforms is disrupting conventional approaches to the sharing of our scholarly voice. It also impacts the measurement and role of altimetric in the growing digitised world (Cabrera et al., 2018).

2.4   Moving beyond journal publication towards a digital context

There are several ways in which we can raise our profile in a digital world. The following examples are by no means exhaustive, but serve as a platform to consider ways suitable for the personal needs and preferences of individuals.

2.4.1   *The affordances of social media in scientific knowledge dissemination*

Social media transformed academe through the breadth and depth of what could be shared and to whom it could be shared. Social media is defined as "the compendium of electronic platforms allowing the creation, curation, and exchange of information in multiple formats and with varying degrees of connectedness, privacy, and accessibility" (Cabrera et al., 2018, p. 135).

Naturally our professional identity could be impacted by the use of digital platforms such as social media. For instance, it provides opportunity for us to become more open about our findings; our visibility to a broader audience is enlarged; there are opportunities to improve our professional identity and chances exist for the creation of online communities (Cabrera et al., 2018; Manca & Ranieri, 2016). The facilitation of conversation about scientific or scholarly findings via social media provides prospects for internal and external knowledge transfer which engages the broader public more (Collins, Shiffman, & Rock, 2016). Social media platforms therefore promote an approach towards the democratisation of knowledge management whereby we have the opportunity to generate, distribute and discuss knowledge in an online domain (Cabrera et al., 2018).

There are numerous social media platforms for us to choose from. These include, for instance, Facebook and Twitter, and then what are often referred to as academic networking sites (ANS) such as LinkedIn, ResearchGate, Academica.eu and so forth. These platforms all afford us different opportunities to create and share knowledge.

2.4.2 *Social media platforms*

Facebook is often used to 'follow' certain pages related to a particular topic or field of interest or, alternatively, administering a page or closed group that specialises in a particular knowledge field. One of the critical questions is how we would perceive the level of scientific narrative in the use of such platforms – especially if one of the aims is to communicate scientific findings to a broader 'layman's' audience.

Twitter provides the opportunity for us to communicate with a large audience (i.e., accumulating Twitter followers) via personal tweets, reposting tweets or to follow other Twitter users. The question to consider is how 'scientific' tweets are and if that is the main purpose of the use of such a microblogging platform. To be considered as scientific tweets, Weller (2011) (as cited in Collins et al., 2016) posit the following points of consideration:

✓ The tweet has scientific gravitas.
✓ The tweet represents the voice of a scientist.
✓ The tweet includes at least one science-related hashtag (can adapt this for broader scholarly community).

Apart from purely scientific perspectives, it seems as if academics/scholars prefer the use of Twitter to communicate with colleagues representing their respective fields of knowledge as well as the sharing of peer-reviewed literature on chosen topics (Collins et al., 2016). Similarly, LinkedIn is a network for all professionals and not only academics, where you have the opportunity to disseminate scholarly ideas, to start online discussions and to participate in groups that are interested in a specific topic. Whichever platforms are preferred, it will make sense for us to consider our social media agenda and the rationale for thinking about these avenues.

There are a number of reasons why we tiptoe around social media and are reluctant to share our scientific findings on a social platform. These reasons include:

✓ A lack of time.
✓ It doesn't suggest that same status as high IF journals.
✓ Limited recognition is given to such approaches.
✓ The lack of the basic skills of setting up and using such platforms.
✓ Some of the journals restrict authors in disseminating their findings in such a manner.
✓ The media might misunderstand or misinterpret the findings of the work.

✓ There is limited evidence of the measurement of research quality in the social media space which impacts the perceived quality of the work shared (Midgley, Nicholson, & Brennan, 2017).

2.4.3 Academic social networking

Closely aligned with 'conventional' social media, another site of disruption in scholarly writing is academic social networks (ASN) which refers to platforms affording us the opportunity to share, search and recover scholarly articles. For the purpose of this chapter, other social media sites such as Facebook and Twitter are not included under the umbrella term of ASNs since they were not specifically developed for academic use and they do not afford authors the chance to store publications in an orderly manner (Laakso et al., 2017).

ASNs are fundamentally designed to offer authors the opportunity to augment their profiles as scholars and to be more detectable by other interested role players, and could inevitably lead to increased citations (Duffy & Pooley, 2017; Laakso et al., 2017). Such platforms include ResearchGate and Academia.edu where readers can download articles of interest. Other ASNs such as Mendeley, Zotero etc. do display similarities to ResearchGate and Academia.edu such as the creation of an online community, authors being able to list their scholarly work, the sharing of work and the creation of an online profile. However, the latter do not afford readers the opportunity to download work they are interested in (Laakso et al., 2017). The main principle of ASN platforms such as Academia or ResearchGate is that users (i.e., academic authors) create content that is of interest to other users who will then also reciprocate with such practices. Such platforms usually attract two groups, namely authors (academics) and then readers of academic or scholarly work. Clearly these two audiences could intersect, but both are afforded the opportunity to select relevant writings, bookmark, post, follow and recommend (Duffy & Pooley, 2017).

An interesting way of considering social media is to think of it as:
✓ Circulation of advertisements
✓ Distribution of developmental work for feedback
✓ Joint writing activities
✓ Exploration of particular scholarly resources via a method of crowd-sourcing (p. 65) (Manca & Ranieri, 2016).

2.4.4 Academic blogging

Another possibility for academics is the consideration of academic blogging. Academic blogging paves the way for us to evolve into so-called 'public intellectuals' by disseminating intellectual thought and discourse to a wider public and varied public audience (Veletsianos, 2013). The academic blog is an online platform utilised by active researchers which focuses on their own current scholarly work. With the use of recontextualisation (Bernstein, 1990), academics create an opportunity for their work to be 'rewritten' for a broader audience and other contexts. One of the advantages of academic blogs is that we democratise our work for a broader audience, provide opportunity for online conversation and debate and to construct a digital platform that could serve as an online community of practice (Zou & Hyland, 2019).

Academic blogs require of us to consider alternative ways of sharing our research and to reflect on the way in which we convey these findings and deliberations to a broader audience. These approaches are often in contrast with the usual strategies we use in terms of being "more reserved" and displaying more "author-evacuated conventions" of the traditional ways of scholarly communication (Zou & Hyland, 2019, p. 2).

2.4.5 The digital portfolio: An integrative approach to scientific authorship

Increasingly academics are encouraged to organise their work into meaningful portfolios that could be disseminated to appropriate audiences such as providing evidence for scholarships, grants and promotion. Electronic portfolios offer a platform not only to share conventional academic contributions, but also to include a body of work that are digitised in nature. In a typical portfolio, academics share their educational philosophy, evidence of various activities, reference to the quality and impact of such activities as well as an opportunity to reflect (Cabrera et al., 2018).

In terms of emphasis placed on the scholarship practices of academics, a social media scholarship portfolio (or alternatively, a section dedicated to it in an electronic portfolio) could demonstrate alternative modes of sharing our scholarly voice. There are several aspects to be considered when developing a social media scholarship portfolio. For instance, attention can be paid to highlighting the author's academic area of expertise, who the targeted audience is and an outline of the different digital platforms that are used. It is also valuable to attempt to align social media scholarly practices with overarching career development plans of the portfolio author. Other aspects that could be included are an overview of the various social media activities, links to examples of scholarly work and metrics associated with scholarly activities.

It is clear that we have multiple choices in disseminating our work to the broader community. Due to the existing nature of HE institutions in terms of intellectual standing, tenure and promotion, publication of scientific work in reputable journals with high impact factors is still a main priority for scholars. Yet, potential avenues to be explored through open access cannot be ignored.

The popularity of social media, and then in particular academic social media networks, creates further opportunity for engagement with scientific work at different levels:

Horizontal: Paper-based vs digital
Vertical: Peer-reviewed vs open access

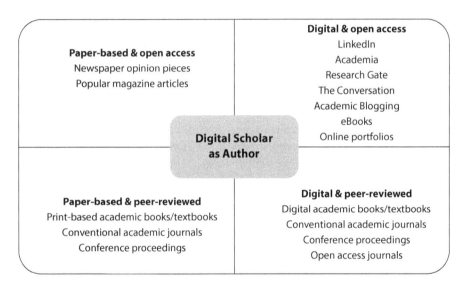

Figure 2.2: Overview of platforms for sharing the scholarly voice.

Case study
Academics use various approaches in communicating their scientific ideas and to promote their own work in online spaces. The following case study by Professor Michael Rowe demonstrates the manner in which the internet is used in the promotion of his scholarly work.

Case Study: The use of the internet to promote scholarship in Physiotherapy

Prof Michael Rowe (Cape Peninsula University of Technology, South Africa)
The use of the internet to promote scholarship in Physiotherapy

This short vignette presents a short perspective of scholarly practice using the web as an alternative to journal publication. The dominant view of *scholarship* is that it describes the output of a process that is published in a peer-reviewed journal. This paradigm has become so dominant that academics tend to equate 'scholarship' with 'publication' and as a result enter into a cycle where 'scholarship' = 'articles'. But this has the result of causing us to miss out on the many different opportunities to share scholarly practice across a more creative spectrum of activities, and also explore the *practice* of scholarship as something that might be shared in community.

If we consider a broad definition of scholarship that includes the practice of discovering and sharing creative ideas that aim to help others solve problems that they care about and that includes a process of critical review, it is clear that 'publication of journal articles' is not a requirement. That just happens to be the format we've accepted as the default. Indeed, even though Ernest Boyer's now 30-year-old report aimed to present a range of scholarly activities, academics still cling to the idea that *scholarship* relates solely to what Boyer called the *scholarship of discovery*; the process of conducting original research as part of the search for new knowledge. And even though we pay lip service to the scholarship of integration, application, and teaching, it is the publication of articles (and successful funding grant applications) that tends to be rewarded in the academy.

But we can still think of the practice of scholarship as much more than journal publication by taking advantage of the tools and platforms available in online and networked communities. If peer-reviewed articles are proxy indicators of our ability to influence the thinking of other people, then impact factors and one's h-index are quite blunt instruments for evaluating this ability. We should acknowledge that publishing articles is a means to an end but not the end in itself. If all we're doing is publishing articles that don't get read, or that don't meaningfully influence the thinking of others, then it serves no real purpose.

Distribution and discovery
When we think of scholarship as a set of practices that revolve around sharing ideas (rather than sharing PDFs) we can start to see what alternatives might look like. The following table provides a rough comparison between two different ways of sharing ideas.

Journals (sharing PDFs)	Web (sharing ideas)
Accreditation (credibility via peer review and legacy)	Accreditation (search engine results ranked by authority and relevance)
Distribution (moving paper around the world is expensive)	Distribution (anyone can publish almost for free)
Artificial scarcity via rejection	Abundance (results aren't limited to specific services)
Peer review is limited and opaque	Peer review is broad and transparent
Siloing of ideas (ideas from one article are disconnected from ideas in other articles (not to mention from other journals)	Networked ideas via hyperlinks (ideas are connected)
Sharing is delayed by journal publication cadence	Publication can happen immediately
No attempt to embed meaning (other than basic keyword search)	Semantic structure embedded in the content (search engines are increasingly able to parse meaning in text)
Publishers demand the intellectual property of the author	The author retains their intellectual property
PDF (static, unstructured data, text and images)	HTML/XML (dynamic, un/structured data, multimedia)
You have to go to them	Sends you to other places

Taking the above into account, we begin to see the potential for the open web to take the place of journals as a primary means of discovery for sharing and finding news ideas. And when the web is the channel of communication rather than the journal, it opens up a world of possibility. The TCP/IP protocol is an open standard, which means that anyone can create new tools and services on top of what already exists. And 'value' is determined by the user not the publisher.

Using the web to share ideas as part of scholarly practice
Based on the previous,
1. Gather 3-5 people together online. They might be experts, or not.
2. Pose a few questions and have the group discuss them. Record it all.
3. Afterwards, analyse the discussion and interpret what the group discussed. This could even be done collaboratively and in public.
4. Record an audio introduction where you explain what led to the questions and what the purpose of the discussion was, as well as a post-script where you explain your analysis and findings.
5. Edit the audio segments together and publish as a podcast.
6. Include links to additional readings and some detailed background and context, published as the podcast show notes.
7. Welcome critical comments from the community and respond to those comments in subsequent episodes.

These activities look a bit like a focus group discussion with analysis and opportunities for critique. I imagine that there are many such discussions taking place among colleagues already but none of these are considered *scholarship* because they don't result in the publication of an article. However, with a little bit of extra effort, I think it's possible for podcasts that follow a certain process to be recognized as scholarly outputs.

Conclusion
We tend to think of peer-reviewed articles as the endpoint in a research project that started with a formal proposal. But we should remember that articles are merely a means to an end and that we can be more creative about different ways of achieving the same outcomes. Scholarly activity need not be defined by the publication of more PDFs, and in the web, we have an incredible system for sharing creative ideas that allow us to fulfil the requirements of scholarly practice.

2.5   Suggestions for the way forward

✓   Identify the emerging trends of scholarly dissemination in your discipline/field.
✓   Start to experiment with the different scholarly paths of dissemination that align with your digital skills and the targeted audience interested in your work.
✓   Identify any open-access platforms that could legitimise your work and grant your needed exposure of your disciplinary knowledge and/ or skills.

2.6   Conclusion

The world of scholarly authorship in education has been transformed and democratised in recent years with the increased availability of digital platforms. The internet and social platforms have afforded academics various ways to share knowledge and explore alternatives to current practices. It is only recently, however, that these platforms have started to impact our scholarly behaviour in terms of knowledge creation and dissemination.

Authors have choices ranging from the established article publication in paper-based and online journals, to e-books and textbooks, academic social networking platforms and online portfolios. These myriad options pave the way for the consideration of how such choices impact the identity of scholars in the modern educational setting. Capital, that which academics value, is being negotiated in terms of alternative ways of assessing quality, impact and reach.

This chapter explored the numerous opportunities we are afforded in the curation and creation of knowledge in a digitised academic world. Although ample opportunities do exist, it still requires us to cautiously consider our online agenda, the purpose and how it could potentially impact our scholarly work in an ever-evolving academic environment.

References

Cabrera, D., Roy, D., & Chisolm, M. S. (2018). Social Media Scholarship and Alternative Metrics for Academic Promotion and Tenure. *Journal of the American College of Radiology*, *15*(1), 135–141. https://doi.org/10.1016/j.jacr.2017.09.012

Collins, K., Shiffman, D., & Rock, J. (2016). How are scientists using social media in the workplace? *PLoS ONE*, *11*(10), 1–10. https://doi.org/10.1371/journal.pone.0162680

Duffy, B. E., & Pooley, J. D. (2017). "Facebook for Academics": The Convergence of Self-Branding and Social Media Logic on Academia.edu. *Social Media and Society*, *3*(1). https://doi.org/10.1177/2056305117696523

Ebrahim, N. A., Salehi, H., Embi, M. A., Tanha, F. H., Gholizadeh, H., Motahar, S. M., & Ordi, A. (2013). Effective strategies for increasing citation frequency. *International Education Studies*, *6*(11), 93–99. https://doi.org/10.5539/ies.v6n11p93

English, F. W., & Bolton, C. L. (2016). *Bourdieu for educators: Policy and practice*. London: Sage.

Ferrare, J. J., & Apple, M. W. (2015). Field theory and educational practice: Bourdieu and the pedagogic qualities of local field positions in educational contexts. *Cambridge Journal of Education*, *45*(1), 43–59. https://doi.org/10.1080/0305764X.2014.988682

French, A. (2019). Academic writing as identity-work in higher education: forming a 'professional writing in higher education habitus.' *Studies in Higher Education*, *0*(0), 1–13. https://doi.org/10.1080/03075079.2019.1572735

Hildebrandt, K., & Couros, A. (2016). Digital selves, digital scholars: Theorising academic identity in online spaces. *Journal of Applied Social Theory*, *1*(1), 87–100.

Hilgers, M., & Mangez, E. (2015). Introduction to Pierre Bourdieu's theory of social fields. In M. Hilgers & E. Mangez (Eds.), *Bourdieu's theory of social fields: Concepts and applications*. (pp. 1–35). New York, NY: Routledge. Retrieved from http://samples.sainsburysebooks.co.uk/9781317678595_sample_666953.pdf

Laakso, M., Lindman, J., Shen, C., Nyman, L., & Björk, B. C. (2017). Research output availability on academic social networks: implications for stakeholders in academic publishing. *Electronic Markets*, *27*(2), 125–133. https://doi.org/10.1007/s12525-016-0242-1

Manca, S., & Ranieri, M. (2016). "yes for sharing, no for teaching!": Social Media in academic practices. *Internet and Higher Education*, *29*, 63–74. https://doi.org/10.1016/j.iheduc.2015.12.004

Maton, K. (2005). A question of autonomy: Bourdieu's field approach and higher education policy. *Journal of Education Policy*, *20*(6), 687–704. https://doi.org/10.1080/02680930500238861

Midgley, G., Nicholson, J. D., & Brennan, R. (2017). Dealing with challenges to methodological pluralism: The paradigm problem, psychological resistance and cultural barriers. *Industrial Marketing Management*, *62*, 150–159. https://doi.org/10.1016/j.indmarman.2016.08.008

Nicholas, D., Rodríguez-Bravo, B., Watkinson, A., Boukacem-Zeghmouri, C., Herman, E., Xu, J., ... Świgoń, M. (2017). Early career researchers and their publishing and authorship practices. *Learned Publishing*, *30*(3), 205–217. https://doi.org/10.1002/leap.1102

Nygaard, L. P. (2017). Publishing and perishing: an academic literacies framework for investigating research productivity. *Studies in Higher Education*, *42*(3), 519–532. https://doi.org/10.1080/03075079.2015.1058351

Origgi, G., & Ramello, G. B. (2015). Current Dynamics of Scholarly Publishing. *Evaluation Review*, *39*(1), 3–18. https://doi.org/10.1177/0193841X15572017

Peters, M. A., Jandrić, P., Irwin, R., Locke, K., Devine, N., Heraud, R., ... Benade, L. (2016). Towards a philosophy of academic publishing. *Educational Philosophy and Theory*, *48*(14), 1401–1425. https://doi.org/10.1080/00131857.2016.1240987

Shammas, V. L., & Sandberg, S. (2015). Habitus, capital, and conflict: Bringing Bourdieusian field theory to criminology. *Criminology and Criminal Justice*, *16*(2), 195–213. https://doi.org/10.1177/1748895815603774

Vandenberghe, F. (2017). Conference of the Critical Realism Network. In *Critical Realism. Anti-utilitarianism and axiological engagement* (pp. 347–353). Montreal: CAIRN, INFO. https://doi.org/10.3917/rdm.050.0347

Veletsianos, G. (2013). Open practices and identity: Evidence from researchers and educators' social media participation. *British Journal of Educational Technology*, *44*(4), 639–651. https://doi.org/10.1111/bjet.12052

Weller, M. (2018). *The Digital Scholar*. *The Digital Scholar: How technology is transforming scholarly practice* (Vol. 1). London: Bloomsbury Academic. https://doi.org/10.5840/dspl2018111

Zou, H., & Hyland, K. (2019). Reworking research: Interactions in academic articles and blogs. *Discourse Studies*, 146144561986698. https://doi.org/10.1177/1461445619866983

3
The Digital Scholar as Storyteller: Using digital audio in teaching, research and social impact

JP Bosman

In this chapter we focus on

✓ Why the ancient art of storytelling, which uses the power of the human voice, is valuable for teaching, research and social impact practices.

✓ How recorded audio can support the teaching practice by using it in student feedback and assessment for and of learning.

✓ How to (carefully) utilise storytelling as part of research and social impact.

✓ Some practical advice on how to start recording your digital stories.

Keywords: Human voice; storytelling; audio feedback for learning; audio for teaching; audio for research.

3.1   Introduction

We often refuse to accept an idea merely because the tone of voice in which
it has been expressed is unsympathetic to us. – Friedrich Nietzsche

The evolving digital scholar as Storyteller has an audience in mind and wants to convey a clear message. We might even go further and say (nodding at Nietzsche) that the digital scholar also wants to convince and make a rhetorical appeal. Like in the role of the Author the Storyteller remains in control of the scholarly narrative and engages in communication with the audience. The difference is that while the digital scholar as Author is mostly writing for fellow experts, the Storyteller is starting to communicate with a broader audience and needs to create a more memorable, accessible narrative – something the audience (readers or listeners) can connect to and retain. Here we find ourselves in the powerful realms of the story, of the human voice and of the world of audio.

Storytelling is the ancient art of sharing knowledge through the social representation of not just information but also emotion (Joubert, Davis, and Metcalfe 2019). A good story (told well) taps not only into the logical-rational mind of the listener, but also into the emotional mind (Siobáhn McHugh 2014). As such it draws the listener into the Storyteller's world and there engages, confronts and informs him/her through the transformative use of plot, characters, twists, climax and tying up any loose ends. The mind loves stories, and the evolving digital scholar can use this reality to craft creative and world-changing stories around his/her knowledge endeavours and how it might affect the way we see the world, or even how the world functions.

Stories told through (written) words alone can already make a difference to the digital scholar's teaching, research and social impact influence. If the telling of these stories is coupled with a real human voice, then the impact and transformative power of the story are potentially amplified.

This amplification happens because the human voice functions as a mirror to the mind and character of the storyteller. The human ear and mind are so attuned to other humans' voices that it can detect not only the surface meaning of the words in spoken form, but also the deeper, richer meanings, convictions and emotions that are almost impossible to convey with only written words. It also mediates the non-verbal – a pause, a gulp or a breath is often loaded with meaning and insight (McHugh 2014). Cutting edge artificial intelligence research into the human voice goes so far as to suggest that each person has a unique vocal signature, and that one can deduct from a few spoken lines of audio how a person looks, what environment they live in and even which underlying illness a person might have (Singh 2019). It certainly gives the listener a nuanced opportunity to get direct access to the storyteller's feelings, emotions, resolves or uncertainties, and in that way creates a very authentic listening experience: that slight pause indicating that there might be something more the person is not willing to talk about or the sudden rise in excitement or even anger which can become an invitation to suspend disbelief and to open the mind to new possibilities of thinking, acting or being.

3.2 The power of the human voice, audio and the telling of stories

The power of stories and the human performance of them is of course as old as civilisation and part of the human experience since time immemorial, so we have to also ask what is different when digitally producing and broadcasting these audio narratives?

In the excellent FutureLearn[9] course, *The power of podcasting for storytelling*, Siobhán McHugh (McHugh 2020) shares the following reasons why audio is so powerful: (a) audio can capture the intangible aspects of a story and thereby can add authenticity; (b) audio can capture the non-verbal aspects of a story, interview or podcast, thereby mediating a more honest experience that is not as scripted as text or video; (c) audio does not care about or put emphasis on physical attributes such as appearance or mannerisms which allows for empathy and connection; (d) audio creates the best combination of words, sounds, and imagination – listeners co-create the story through imagination and interpretation; and (e) there is an emotional and affective appeal in listening. According to her it's "partly about the temporal nature of sound – unable to jump ahead as in text, or freeze-frame as in film, the listener develops a pact of intimacy with the sound or speaker as the audio unfolds in real time" (McHugh 2020, section 1.4).

Paul Zak talks about audio stories creating a "narrative transportation" (when there is tension in the story and the listener is engulfed in the story because of the release of oxytocin) and a "neuro ballet" in which the "reader, viewer, or listener knows she's not physically part of the story, and yet she still physically responds to it in a way that can change her behaviour in the future" (Wen 2015).

The telling of stories, especially when done through the medium of audio, is something evolving digital scholars can therefore utilise to their advantage. In the world of teaching, audio and stories can create more effective active learning, student engagement and especially a way to provide critically important student feedback. In the realm of research, the process and product of the scholar's scientific contributions can be bolstered by storytelling (although there might be a slight caveat). For social impact, the telling of scholarly socially significant stories, amplified through excitement, urgency and deep love for a discipline, has the potential to fight fake science and news and to transform society and the world.

3.3   Using audio in Teaching and Learning

The first and most prominent use of audio in teaching is the creation of powerful cumulative knowledge-building[10] resources. The second has to do with assessment for and of student learning.

3.3.1   *Creating audio teaching resources*

The digital scholar as Storyteller can add an important (maybe missing) layer to teaching as he/she creates short, concise, personality-infused, similar-to-stories lectures, talks or even podcasts. As we will see in Chapter 5, integrating multimedia draws on Universal Design for Learning (UD4L) principles and underlines the importance of creating audio and written transcripts when you publish a video. So, audio plays a very important role in providing access to visually impaired students – especially if the audio of the video contains descriptions of the important non-verbal video elements. But here we are talking about creating an audio-based learning experience which is also not reading your notes verbatim into a microphone. Of course, UD4L best practice calls for the creation of a transcript of that audio-experience.

In terms of UD4L, audio is one of the distinguishing factors towards creating accessible educational resources, not only in terms of disabilities, but also as a more equitable low-data usage strategy. Audio resources could include short lectures to explain threshold concepts, short introductory notes to a new topic by giving an overview of what to expect, a short introduction of yourself to your students at the start of an online course, or a discussion forum post only in audio with you inviting your students to respond in audio. It could also be posting a radio interview with yourself on the topic at hand, an interview or even a dialogue with an expert in your field.

This could of course be done quite flexibly and on the fly. Our smart phones typically have very capable microphones, and using the built-in or specialised recording apps we can easily share an audio post on the learning management system (LMS) discussion forum while standing in line at the pharmacy or record an impromptu interview with an expert you bump into in a coffee shop. You could record urban or rural sounds, animals, people, trees swaying in the wind, machines – anything that could become interesting and authentic material for teaching your subject.

Once the audio-bug has bitten, however, many digital scholars 'up' their recording 'game' by investing in a decent microphone, headphones and even a little audio-mixer and consider improving the sound dampening profile of their home office[11]. If you want to take it even further you can find out if your institution has a recording studio (with excellent sound-dampening as well as high quality microphones) that you can use, or if your institution's learning spaces have high end audio equipment (or even cameras) so that you could 'perform' your lecture/ talk or message in that space and record the audio and video.

And then you could start by creating your own podcasting channel …

3.3.2 Using recorded audio feedback in assessment for and of student learning[12]

Recorded audio feedback (RAF) can be a powerful tool *for* (formative) as well as *of* (summative) learning, as we know that high quality feedback positively impacts student performance. When we realise that our students prefer audio rather than written feedback, it is an approach one probably should explore. Hayman found in his study of sport coaching students that 79% students listened to his audio feedback within 60 minutes and only 6% preferred written feedback (Hayman 2020). It can also contribute to rapid student engagement and an enhanced student experience. Looking at the use of recorded audio feedback (RAF) in cross-cultural e-education environments, Heimbürger (2018, p.108) concludes that:

> "audio feedback has also been noted as bridging a gap between the learner and the supervisor and being a time-saver for the supervisor … With RAF, supervisors can use clear and effective, often less technical, language in order to convey their message to learners. Specific subject-related vocabulary can be explained in a more conversational style or uncomplicated manner than it can be in written format. RAF is often more nuanced than written feedback, with meanings being derived not only from the spoken words but also from the tone of voice, which can be used to convey an overall impression of the feedback."

The value of audio feedback lies in the fact that it is possible to give more in-depth responses and more personal feedback than in written feedback.

It also has the potential to create the perception of care and support and so contributes to the humanising of online learning. Furthermore, it can move away from only focusing on problematic aspects and indicate ways to improve a student's work, and has the potential for clearer and less ambiguous feedback (McCarthy 2015).

Case study: Audio feedback in a Blended Learning Short Course

At Stellenbosch University we offer an *Introduction to Blended Teaching and Learning* short course and participants have to complete a capstone project to obtain a certificate. The submissions are made on our LMS and graded with a rubric and open comments. To create a more personalised constructive formative form of feedback we started giving audio feedback on the assignments by either recording it in Audacity (or on a smartphone) and uploading the audio file against the participant's submission or using the built-in audio recorder in the LMS. The participant feedback on this way of giving academic feedback has always surprised us. The lecturers love getting such personalised comments which connect them to their teaching practice, their faculty and our shared institution. As such they are not just getting a grade but getting a kind of invitation to join the institutional community of practice around blended learning practice. How to give such audio feedback has become fairly easy in our digital world of which higher education is part and parcel. Most modern Learning Management Systems (like Moodle, Blackboard and Canvas) have the ability to create audio recordings within the editor application, or as part of the feedback options when grading students' assignments. You basically need a laptop, enable/ allow use of the microphone, and then press record, stop and then save or submit the recording into the discussion forum or assignment tool. If the LMS itself does not have built-in recording functionalities there are many ways to record your feedback on your laptop or smart phone, with native or special voice recording applications. You record the audio on the device, save the audio file (usually in .mp3 format as that creates the smallest file size which can play across all devices) and upload it into the LMS at the point of feedback.

Another way of giving audio feedback is to insert your audio notes directly onto a student's document. In Microsoft Word it is now possible to insert audio notes that you record directly while in the application. You save the audio notes with the file and send them to the student. With Adobe PDF reader it is also possible to add audio notes for feedback (or even when you want to make audio annotations on a journal article). Finally, you could even record your audio feedback and send it as an e-mail attachment, a WhatsApp message or Microsoft Teams voice note to the student.

These are all teacher-led RAF activities, but you could of course open this exciting world of audio to your students as well. You could have *them* make podcast series (in teams), develop digital stories, do oral exams over Microsoft Teams, Zoom or Skype, record field notes and interviews with experts, or take part in audio-based discussions on the LMS.

This is an expanding field of digital educational practice and one that is worth investing time and energy in!

3.3.3 Creating Digital Stories for student engagement and reflection

Although not a direct practice of the EDS, the use of digital story-creation by students for assessment and learning has become a powerful strategy to further student engagement and especially reflection: "digital storytelling provides a potentially powerful tool for rethinking and supporting assessment practices in higher education, which can lead to students acquiring high-level reflection, and as a result lead to deep learning and development of higher-order thinking skills" (Ivala et al. 2013, p.224).

Case study: Digital (video) stories on plant propagation and nursery design

For years now Dr. Michael Schmeisser, a Stellenbosch University Hortology lecturer, has been asking his second year Crop Production students to create digital story movies around plant propagation and nursery design. Michael's case study concludes regarding the stories: "Although digital stories have not yet been used extensively in scientific fields, with some modifications, the digital movie format is an effective way to take students through the process of engaging with content and presenting it in a concise way. The students do engage with the information and find the process more interesting than traditional lectures, feeling that they learnt more about the topic than they expected. The movies that are produced are highly creative and diverse and students who are not academically strong can do well in this project. Many students go beyond the scope of the project guidelines, adapting the project to their own interests. The project is also very authentic in terms of the way that the question is asked, the requirement for a business proposal and the presentation of the work in a format that is interesting" (CLT 2016, p.3).

StoryCenter[13] provides a wealth of information as well as workshops (and of course stories as well) on the creation of digital stories for the EDS to peruse and apply.

3.4. Research and social impact perspectives on storytelling

This section brings us into the realm of science communication and how stories (and audio then of course) can support the peer and public understanding of your research and the implications thereof. Joubert, Davis and Metcalfe (Joubert, Davis & Metcalfe 2019, p.1) call storytelling the "soul of science communication":

> "In a world where we increasingly look towards science and technology to find answers that will help us secure a fair and sustainable future, it is imperative that people become empowered to make informed decisions about issues rooted in science. To achieve this, science communicators must make science-related information engaging and relevant. In short, it is about making people care. That is why we need to go beyond presenting facts and evidence, towards creating emotional connections between scientists and publics."

Suzuki et al. (2018, p.9468) concur on the value and persuasive use of stories: "It is now more urgent than ever that scientists take an active role in engaging with and educating the public about what they do as scientists, why they do it, and why it matters. It is in this context that many scientists hear about the craft of storytelling." They go on to talk about how the backstory behind how a research question was born is often as interesting as the data the study generate as it serves in the "meaningful transfer of knowledge because it elicits participation and creates an intellectual investment and emotional bond between the speaker and the audience" (Suzuki et al. 2018, p.9468).

It, however, seems to be more a case of using the strategy when engaging non-expert audiences and that a narrative approach could offer "increased comprehension, interest, and engagement" (Dahlstrom 2014, p.13614). For storytelling to scientific expert peers, the critical opinion of Katz should be kept in mind as one of the dangers of scientific writing following journalistic 'storytelling' is that "the choice of what data to plot, and how, is tailored to the message the authors want to deliver" and the pitfalls of an approach and the "experimental complexities and their myriad of interpretations" are sanitised (Katz 2013, p.1045).

In the very practical handbook, *Research: How do you get it out there?* (De Haardt and Van de Water 2015), five reasons are given why one should publicise or communicate about one's research more: (1) more support (and possibly more funding); (2) widen one's network; (3) makes one more accountable (when using public funds e.g.); (4) it provides satisfaction to the researcher; and (5) one is not alone in that there is help available. The authors then provide lots of very useful tips and tricks for successfully using different kinds of media/storytelling approaches: from how to make sure your story has a "wow" factor and how you get into the media, to how to look for support and assistance at your own institution and tips from experts on press releases, presentations, TV or radio interviews, taking photos, making scientific posters, social media, and video. It is well worth the read!

3.5 How to record, edit and publish good audio

Since we have touched upon some of the basics of recording for teaching and learning (focussed on the LMS) in the above section, we will briefly provide some pointers and practical tips for starting with high quality audio recording. We mention high quality because in a multimedia project, audio is the most important part to get right. You could have a great video or animation, or your story could be gripping, but if something is "off" with the audio (too soft, background noise, hissing, too loud etc. – therefore, anything that disrupts the quality of the audio) it diminishes the impact of that resource. High quality is of course not only technical (like a clean and clear and well-balanced sound) but also the quality of your presentation. You should be excited about (or at least sound interested in) your own research or topic or how you give feedback. As we have learned, the human ear and mind can pick up the tiniest of nuances in the voice, which includes non-verbal aspects of boredom, uncertainty or even hostility. So, before you switch on your microphone and press the record button, be sure to prepare your voice, mind and attitude for the task at hand!

Microphones are central to the quality of your recording and the price of the microphone is most often a reflection of its quality (the more expensive the better the sound). To start off, you could invest in a good quality USB headset. Then you could possibly consider a podcasting microphone (usually a bit more expensive and comes with more audio settings) and then an audio-mixer. As we have already mentioned, do not discard your smartphone as an option. Some high-end smart phones have excellent microphones and if one buys a microphone that can plug into the phone, one can reach quite high sound recording quality. High end laptops also have decent microphones, and as an evolving digital scholar one could experiment with that and see if the quality of the recording fits the need for the recording. What we mean is that not all recordings need to be perfect. A quick voice note for the discussion forum could be made on the laptop microphone and sent off without thinking (or even editing). Your next podcasting recording, however, needs more attention with regard to the microphone and the environment one records in as well as editing of the raw recording.

Where one records can make a big difference and it (hopefully) goes without saying that recording in an open office or in one's kitchen while the pasta is boiling on the stove and the cat is interested in walking on your keyboard is not conducive to a good quality sound recording. Find a place as quiet as possible where one will not be disturbed (especially where there is no air-conditioning, or where the air-conditioning can be switched off). Do test recordings, and if one has control over the levels of the incoming audio from the microphone experiment until the sound is acceptable (remember the human ear is the best quality assurance instrument – if one doesn't like it, others probably will not either). If the room is sparce (no chairs with cushions, or a wooden floor, or no curtains e.g.) the sound quality could be hollow and could be improved by putting sound dampening items in the room (like cushions or blankets over the cupboard door). We have even gone so far as to throw a thick blanket over your head and the computer to create a sound-proof little (very hot) recording space!

Software to record is also not a hurdle as the modern operating systems (like Windows 10 – Voice recorder and Apple Mac OS – QuickTime) come equipped with recording applications. Mac even added a (pay for subscription) native application *Podcast Studio* to its newest version. Then there are the free powerful tools like Audacity and Garage band and moving to more paid-for and expert packages you could consider Camtasia Studio or Adobe Audition.[14] Smart phone apps include AudioCopy (for iOS) and Soundcloud (for Android) as well as a myriad of other apps like Hindenburg. And if one has internet access one can easily record one's audio directly in the internet browser at services like Otter or Cleanfeed. Otter will even create a transcript of your audio automatically![15]

Where to host your audio is also straight forward. There are open platforms that are free up to a certain amount of storage, like Soundcloud, Anchor or even Google Drive. Google has its own podcast service, and so does Apple (with iTunes Podcasts). One could also use YouTube or any of the many podcasting services available.[16]

3.6   Suggested way forward

✓   Start focusing on finding excellent stories (especially academic related ones in your discipline) or listening to podcasts that can give you a vision of the quality and depth that is possible with telling powerful stories for teaching, research or social impact.

✓   Start making digital stories yourself. Are you ready? Find somewhere quiet and open your phone's voice recorder. Think about the following question: *How can I use audio to teach more creatively in my subject?* Order your thoughts about it and then record your response, trying to remember all the good things about audio and the human voice that you have just read and maybe choose one of the ideas that was shared. Congratulations (if) you have made your first voice recording! Now make yourself heard ...

3.7   Final thoughts on audio and stories

Words mean more than what is set down on paper. It takes the human voice to infuse them with deeper meaning – Maya Angelo

Evolving one's written work as evolving digital scholar Author by complementing (or replacing some of) it with one's own and other powerful human voices, intentionally recorded to teach, or communicate, or influence, or transform, or build knowledge, is an invitation to awaken the storyteller inside.

Evolving or growing as digital storyteller or digital story-enabler probably follows the route of starting small with your own course or small research project for your own students and then growing from there. One can grow technically by acquiring better recording equipment and improving one's recording environment and immersing oneself in the "physics" side of sound and sound engineering. Conceptually, you grow by trying different genres of audio, story and the power of interviews and podcasts, becoming good at it and then trying something new. Scholarly you evolve by being a reflective practitioner on your digital audio storytelling teaching and science-communication endeavours and sharing those reflective insights through telling your story at seminars, conferences or any form of publication. Finally, you grow by combining human voice forces with a colleague or co-researcher to enable your transformative educational message to be heard and celebrated on an open and global platform!

References

CLT. 2016. "Blended Learning Case Studies 2016." Stellenbosch: Centre for Learning Technologies, Stellenbosch University. http://www.sun.ac.za/english/learning-teaching/learning-teaching-enhancement/learning-technologies/Documents/Case_Studies_2016/BLCS 2016 Online Full Version.pdf.

Dahlstrom, Michael F. 2014. "Using Narratives and Storytelling to Communicate Science with Nonexpert Audiences." *Proceedings of the National Academy of Sciences of the United States of America* 111: 13614–20. https://doi.org/10.1073/pnas.1320645111.

Haardt, Lisa De, and Hans Van de Water. 2015. *Research: How Do You Get It out There?* Brussel: Kristien Verbrugghen. https://cdn.vliruos.be/vliruos/d0b992a9ef88038ddee8c7ed-d9edb985.pdf.

Hayman, Rick. 2020. "Practice and Evidence of Scholarship of Teaching and Learning in Higher Education." Vol. 14.

Heimbürger, Anneli. 2018. "Using Recorded Audio Feedback in Cross-Cultural e-Education Environments to Enhance Assessment Practices in a Higher Education." *Advances in Applied Sociology* 08 (02): 106–24. https://doi.org/10.4236/aasoci.2018.82007.

Ivala, Eunice, Daniela Gachago, Janet Condy, and Agnes Chigona. 2013. "Digital Storytelling and Reflection in Higher Education: A Case of Pre-Service Student Teachers and Their Lecturers at a University of Technology." *Journal of Education and Training Studies* 2 (1): 217–27. https://doi.org/10.11114/jets.v2i1.286.

Joubert, Marina, Lloyd Davis, and Jenni Metcalfe. 2019. "Storytelling: The Soul of Science Communication." *Journal of Science Communication* 18 (5): 1–5. https://doi.org/10.22323/2.18050501.

Katz, Yarden. 2013. "Against Storytelling of Scientific Results." *Nature Methods* 10 (11): 1045. https://doi.org/10.1038/nmeth.2699.

McCarthy, Josh. 2015. "Evaluating Written, Audio and Video Feedback in Higher Education Summative Assessment Tasks." *Issues in Educational Research* 25 (2): 153–69.

McHugh, Siobáhn. 2014. "Listen up: 10 Tips for Using Audio in Storytelling amid the Podcasting Renaissance." World News Publishing Focus. 2014. https://blog.wan-ifra.org/2014/11/03/listen-up-10-tips-for-using-audio-in-storytelling-amid-the-podcasting-renaissance.

McHugh, Siobhán. 2020. "The Power of Podcasting for Storytelling." FutureLearn Course. 2020. www.futurelearn.com.

Singh, Rita. 2019. *Profiling Humans from Their Voice*. Singapore: Springer Nature.

Suzuki, Wendy A., Mónica I. Feliú-Mójer, Uri Hasson, Rachel Yehuda, and Jean Mary Zarate. 2018. "Dialogues: The Science and Power of Storytelling." *Journal of Neuroscience* 38 (44): 9468–70. https://doi.org/10.1523/JNEUROSCI.1942-18.2018.

Wen, Tiffanie. 2015. "Inside the Podcast Brain: Why Do Audio Stories Captivate? The Emotional Appeal of Listening." The Atlantic. 2015. https://www.theatlantic.com/entertainment/archive/2015/04/podcast-brain-why-do-audio-stories-captivate/389925/.

4
The Digital Scholar as Creator: Integrating digital media design with scholarly practice

Miné de Klerk

In this chapter we focus on

- ✓ The argument for and against scholars adopting the role of 'creator'.
- ✓ The types of creative outputs that can be generated, using accessible and affordable tools, to support teaching and research endeavours.
- ✓ The creation of multimedia artefacts as an act of service, to address the needs of the end-user.
- ✓ A framework for starting any creative project in a scholarly environment, based on the context of the creator, their project and their intended audience.
- ✓ An approach for planning the content or message, for choosing the most appropriate digital medium and for planning the design process.

Key words: Digital multimedia; design and development; creative outputs for scholarship; digital academic resources; content strategy; content planning; creative projects.

4.1   Introduction

The role of a scholar can intuitively be likened to that of an 'author' or 'storyteller', as outlined in previous chapters of this book. These roles involve tasks and responsibilities that are typically part of the scholarly practice, such as disseminating research findings, articulating academic arguments and bridging (multi-)disciplinary perspectives.

As an 'author' capturing one's observations and circulating scholarship may occur through a multitude of formats, although the more familiar, text-based medium is still most closely associated with (academic) authorship.[17] The use of narrative to convey complex information, as in the case of the 'storyteller',[18] should also be familiar to anybody that has engaged in teaching or science communication for broader, public audiences. TED talks[19] and audio podcasts are, for instance, common examples. The role of a (digital) *Creator*, however, tends to seem less aligned with our traditional notion of the scholar. It implies that one would need to develop the technical skills to not only curate, evaluate and engage with multimedia but also to actively use information and communication technologies (ICTs) to *produce* digital resources.

Learning new technical skills may understandably cause some trepidation. Creating digital media is an undeniably practical undertaking that calls for either prior technical knowledge and experience, financial resources to outsource these skills, or the support and patience to acquire the necessary skills ourselves. For scholars in particular, content creation is not deemed a central part of their role. Creating a video resource of a lecture, for instance, should not be equated to the facilitation of learning – as argued by David Kellerman (2021) in a widely shared *Times Higher Education* article. In the midst of the global COVID-19 pandemic, Kellerman rightly pointed out that academics were being expected to spend more time on editing videos than to engage with their students, resulting in an abundance of (not necessarily high quality) resources that do not replace the guidance, dialogue and mentorship that students require. Indeed, the world is not in need of more digital content for content's sake. We are drowning in (not necessarily accurate or complete) information, which is often disseminated to furthering profit-seeking or political agendas. Rather, scholars should engage in content-creation and information-sharing to balance and improve how information is shared, so that it can lead to critical thinking, learning and progress. So, as evolving digital scholars, we will always be curating, adapting and recreating high-quality content. To do so in an increasingly digital word, we further need to identify the most appropriate and effective information-dissemination tools at our disposal.

The ability to create original digital artefacts that contribute to critical think-ing, learning and progress poses a number of attractive advantages for not only teachers, but also researchers. It enables one to leverage multiple senses – sight, sound and even touch – to augment how one's work is communicated to a wider audience. Many scholars have, of course, approached the creation of digital resources not necessarily as an activity to engage in themselves, but rather as the subject of intellectual interest. One can argue that scholars would be more inclined to study or observe multimedia design, as opposed to devel-oping multimedia themselves. This is reflected in the rich body of knowledge on the topic (See: *Table 4.1*) spanning various focal areas across multiple dis-ciplines. This provides us with a helpful starting point for creative projects, as well as frameworks for reflection and evaluation during and after the process. That said, theoretical lenses cannot (nor are these intended to) equip us with the digital design skills that can only be acquired through practical experience.

For the 'first-time' creator the thought of multimedia production will most likely seem like an inordinately technical challenge. The very word 'create' signals a practical act, somewhat at odds with our conventional notions of the cerebral predispositions of the scholar. The term 'create' originates from the Latin *creātus*, the perfect passive participle of *creō*, meaning "to bring some-thing specific into existence", "to make "or "to produce". And yet, the process of creation is undoubtedly an inherent part of the contemporary scholar's role – embedded both in academic labour and professional practice. For example, the evolution of digital humanities in recent years is proving that critical lit-eracy can transcend the study of texts, and digital visualisations are increas-ingly accepted as means to make legitimate scholarly arguments (Champion, 2016). In other disciplines, including the natural sciences, video, audio, imagery and multi-sensory experiences can make scholarly works more per-suasive and compelling, and have been shown to widen the reach and societal impact of research outputs (Sayers, 2018). Digital media have further become so ubiquitous and vernacular in contemporary society that video clips, audio podcasts, virtual animations and other online resources offer highly effective vehicles for knowledge production (Dezuanni, 2015). If the digital scholar's objective is to actively participate in and serve contemporary society, to com-municate research findings and facilitate learning. Digital media is no longer a mere add-on – it is a shared language with many emerging dialects.

It is further interesting to note that the origin of the Latin verb 'create' (*creātus*) is very closely related to *crescere*, which broadly means 'to arise, to increase' or 'to grow'. For the purposes of this chapter we will apply the above-mentioned interpretation of the notion of 'creation'. Creating a digital artefact does not have to be motivated solely by the goal of delivering a single output. Rather, any practical attempt at digital creation – whether we deem it successful or not – can serve as a stimulus to evolve all dimensions of our digital scholarship (i.e., our position as 'authors', 'storytellers', 'networkers' or 'integrators'). A single infographic or video clip can, for instance, plant a seed of curiosity that eventually expands the viewers' interest in another topic or academic field. From there, an iterative process of dialogue and learning – on the part of both the 'creator' and the 'audience' – can occur.[20]

4.2   'Creation' in practice

Multimedia permeate our lives, our conscious and subconscious thought through various channels – the smart devices we wear, the advertising bill-boards we pass, our smartphone screens (rarely less than an arm's length away), and the audio broadcasts in public spaces. These sensory channels are not only functional means for exchanging information but are accepted as a reflection of the very structures of our society. If you choose to be intentionally mindful about all the digital media that you perceive or engage with today, you will undoubtedly observe that they reveal much about what our society is choosing to embrace, reject or grapple with, in terms of our present and past. What we see, listen to and read via digital screens is both an explicit product of our cultural inheritance and a clue to what our implicit societal aspirations are.

To function in modern-day society, it is therefore essential that we under-stand how digital media shape our identity. By continually developing the skills to optimally use the digital devices, channels and tools at our disposal, we are taking part in this conversation. Understanding how to create digi-tal media is, in essence, a means of participating in information exchange, and – especially as scholars – we can (co-)create media artefacts to exert agency about what information we consume, how we critically engage with it, and what we choose to communicate to others. In short, as evolving dig-ital scholars, we should be able to critically evaluate the quality and validity of the massive volume of digital data that permeates our lives. That said, we should also challenge ourselves to create (or contribute to) original digital content in order actively to participate in the type of global knowledge pro-duction that aligns with our values (Brown, 2011).

Fortunately, multimedia production tools are becomingly increasingly easy to adopt for novice users, and open-source alternatives are already available to create high-quality media at low or even no cost.[21] As advanced technical skills are no longer required to generate digital media, the possi-bilities for scholars to create media to support their research, teaching and service activities seem unbounded. Consider this suggestion by Anderson and McPherson (2011):

> "While digital scholarship in its simplest form might simply mean publishing traditional work online, we should encourage a variety of approaches and nascent forms that better take advantage of the affordances of computation and allow us to ask new research questions. [Experimental] projects have explored many nascent genres…These forms are not fixed and fast; they can overlap in a project that draws on the multiple capacities of digital media" (p.140).

So, if we accept that digital media genres are not 'fixed and fast', we can conclude that they are emergent in nature. ICTs are continually evolving, and the process of creation is not limited to a single medium. This is not necessarily convenient for those of us who prefer to 'stick with what we know'. It is quite natural to want to hone a particular skillset – such as basic video recording and editing, or infographic design – once we have generated experience in this activity. However, our choice of media should not be primarily informed (however alluringly) by our personal preferences or sense of familiarity, but rather shaped by our *audience's*[22] need. Such an audience-centric approach to digital media creation may be challenging at first, but it opens highly rewarding and unexpected creative avenues.

An audience-centric (or selfless) creative stance calls for the following:

1. An **ongoing exploration** of multiple and emergent digital technologies, along with a willingness **continually to develop relevant technical skillsets to apply and augment these technologies**.
2. The **prioritisation of the imagined audience's context and needs** *above* the creator's personal media- or ICT-related preferences.

We acknowledge how discomforting it can be to envisage starting any creative process with the audience's needs as a point of departure, as opposed to one's own skillset. It seems to suggest a process of technical re-skilling and venturing beyond one's comfort zone of reliable, tried-and-tested digital tools. However, we argue that humans have a marvellous aptitude for acquiring new technological skills on a daily basis – in incremental and intuitive ways. Our use of multiple technological devices is already entangled with our professional and social practices, and we tend to acquire the necessary technical proficiencies to create new media artefacts without even being consciously aware of it (Sayers 2018; Sloman and Fernbach 2018). To illustrate this point, we have created a brief summary of possible professional objectives that could be met through multimedia creation. The majority of scholars would recognise, from a quick scan of the table, that they have in fact engaged in digital media production to some degree:

Digital media creation for research	
Possible objectives: ✓ To interpret complex datasets (Sloman and Fernbach, 2018). ✓ To share or store information amongst research teams (Brown, 2011). ✓ To test the applicability of emerging technical skills and tools for the development of a given academic field (Kaltenbrunner, 2015).	*Examples of what can be created:* ✓ Audio, video and digital image capturing as research artefacts or as tools for participatory research. ✓ Data visualisation of research findings (2D, 3D, immersive, etc.). ✓ Video recordings of experiments or of practical demonstrations. ✓ Simulations to demonstrate functionalities of emerging ICTs. ✓ Cloud-based, open-source or interactive digital repositories.
Digital media creation for teaching	
Possible objectives: ✓ To create interactive resources to facilitate technical skills training (Kaltenbrunner, 2015). ✓ To co-create digital resources with students, fellow teachers or disciplinary/industry experts to better facilitate authentic and industry-relevant learning (Anderson and McPherson, 2011). ✓ To enable academic literacy skills (Dezuanni, 2015). ✓ To use visual graphics to generate interest and more active engagement with learning materials (Xie et al., 2018). ✓ To re-contextualise artefacts and materials in light of your curriculum and/or research activities. (Mark E. Deschaine and Sue Ann Sharma, 2015).	*Examples of what can be created:* ✓ (Interactive) video/audio podcast documentaries. ✓ Virtual simulations related to specific fields of study. ✓ Audio/video interviews (podcasts) with disciplinary experts, industry practitioners and scholars that students may not have general access to. ✓ Recordings of webinars that can be repurposed in different educational formats. ✓ PDFs and other digital text-based files annotated with hyperlinks, bookmarks, audio and text notes. ✓ The application of infographic and graphic design tools to improve understanding of complex concepts that can be better articulated in a visual format. ✓ Digital video material as learning resources.
Digital media creation for service	
Possible objectives: ✓ To generate resources that can be re-applied in a broader variety of contexts, i.e. external to the scholar's institutional role (Kim, Yi, and Cho, 2013). ✓ To share research findings in more accessible ways with the public, and to raise awareness on important research-related topics (Moura, Almeida, and Geerts, 2016). ✓ To contribute to our global understanding of how to critically interrogate and engage with digital media (Parker, 2013).	*Examples of what can be created:* ✓ Downloadable media files, shared on a public platform under an open licence, with guidelines on how the files can be used as resources in another context. ✓ A YouTube or SoundCloud (or other open podcast) channel that features audio podcasts/videos explaining emerging research advances and its potential industry applications. ✓ Research outputs, shared in open and accessible formats (e.g., recorded webinars), that report on the use and application of multimedia within a disciplinary field or teaching context.

Table 4.1: Digital media creation for research, teaching and service: Possible objectives and relevant tools.

The above examples of digital outputs are far from exhaustive. The intention of the summary is to highlight how the creation of digital outputs can be directly informed by the needs and context of a specific (often far from homogenous) group of people. As suggested in the next section of this chapter, the efficacy of the eventual digital product will heavily depend on whether the design was informed by a consideration of *which* message could benefit the audience, as well as *how* the message can reach them.

4.3   A three–tiered approach to digital media creation

There is a vast array of factors that affect multimedia production. In addition to the multitude of ICTs and media genres to consider, the scope of the project can range from the smaller-scale, individual-creator level, to a more complex, team-collaboration level. Whatever the scale of the project, the following broad questions can guide the creator's (or number of co-creators') planning and development processes.

Three questions to consider before embarking on digital media development:

1.) *Why* *do we want to create a digital media product?* This question will inform our **content development** strategy. It is usually aligned to our broader objectives of the value we want to offer our intended audience.

2.) *What* *type of product is it possible to create, whilst meeting the audience's needs?* This question relates to the **choice of ICT (digital software and/or hardware) as well as the media genre.** It is underpinned by the relationship between the project and the audience context, i.e., the alignment and gaps between

   a) the choice of ICTs and the dissemination channel or platform, and

   b) the audience's expected technical aptitude and level of access to the digital channel or platform.

3.) *How* *can we create this?* After interrogating the above, we should consider the **design and development process**. It requires us to acknowledge our own capabilities and role in the project (what we *can* do) in relation to the project context which may be governed by organisational, legislative and technical infrastructure.

As we consider these questions it becomes apparent that there are three overlapping, yet distinct contexts that will inform the answers to these questions: that of the **digital scholar** (as the creator), their **intended audience** (who they want to create for), and the **project** (the parameters of what they can create, on a practical level):[23]

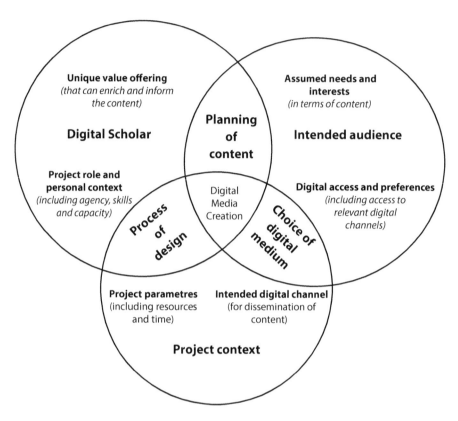

Figure 4.1: Digital Multimedia Creation framework for Scholars.

The **intended audience** is the individuals or groups that will most likely engage with the created product. They may be a group of people that the creator knows on a personal level (e.g., a student cohort or members of a focused interest group) or they may be a much broader segment of the public. The larger the audience, the more one's understanding of it is subject to assumptions. The fewer the assumptions, the more effective the creative product. As members of mass consumer audiences ourselves, we know that the most engaging media content is based on some understanding of an audience's educational needs, areas of interests and knowledge gaps. (Any Netflix subscriber will know that an algorithm that responds to our very niche taste in entertainment can, despite concerns about how our consumer behaviour data are being monetised, be wholly satisfying.) How the content is delivered to the audience is also key: The relevant digital platform needs to be accessible and convenient for the audience.

When adopting the role of the creator, the **digital scholar** should reflect on what s/he can offer (e.g., knowledge production, the facilitation of professional networking or teaching), what can be feasibly achieved given their current and emergent skillset, and which resources can be applied. Access to resources is typically governed by the project context, which usually includes a range of technical, structural and human variables. These implications are explored in more detail later in this chapter.

Finally, there is the **project context.** In some cases, the 'project' can simply be an individual attempt at exploring new ICTs or an informal experiment. However, scholars often create digital resources in a formal, professional context – as part of a collaborative research project, as part of an educational repository for an educational institution, or for a professional networking digital platform (please see Chapter 7 for further details). In these cases, other role players and structures need to be considered before we start creating multimedia. It may be necessary to think about copyright regulations and the risks associated with eventually disseminating the output that has been created. Depending on the project objective or brief, there may be quality requirements and even issues of branding and corporate style guides (should the project be funded or owned by a specific institution/organisation). When generating digital media, we need to remain cognisant of how they will or can be shared, who owns them, how they can be augmented, and how they will be stored, archived or updated.

4.3.1 Planning of content

So often we start our thinking around the creation of multimedia based on a specific technical genre. We tend first to contemplate *what* we want to create, imagining the tangible end-result (e.g., a video, an audio file or a virtually simulated experience). We should, of course, rather start by asking ourselves 'why' we want to create a certain artefact. It is possible that our propensity for starting with the 'tool' as opposed to the 'need' is simply the result of being exposed to – and then responding to – something interesting we observed. One might be drawn to video as a genre after seeing a thought-provoking documentary, or one may start exploring the affordances of audio podcasts after enjoying listening or a particularly well-produced audio series.

Of course, at the very early stages of being exposed to the various affordances of new multimedia tools it makes sense that we follow our own preferences. It is even natural and helpful to explore new multimedia in a curious, unstructured way – when we do not yet have a clear objective in mind in terms of how we can use the same media for professional purposes.

This will change, however, once the decision is made to deliberately create something new for a particular audience and purpose. Once we've committed to intentionally generating a digital artefact that will have some impact and value for an imagined audience, it becomes a creative **project.**

In order to create a project – something meaningful that will contribute to our digital scholarship – we need to momentarily put our personal preferences for a particular media genre aside and start by considering the underlying purpose of our project. *Why are we creating this digital resource? For whom?* A content creation strategy relies on the alignment between a.) the creator's inherent value offering – whether it be their knowledge base, their access to a professional network, or their experience – and b.) the group of people that could benefit from these attributes. The diagram below illustrates this proposed first step in the design process: the intentional articulation of a project purpose, which we can also (more simply) call 'planning of content'.

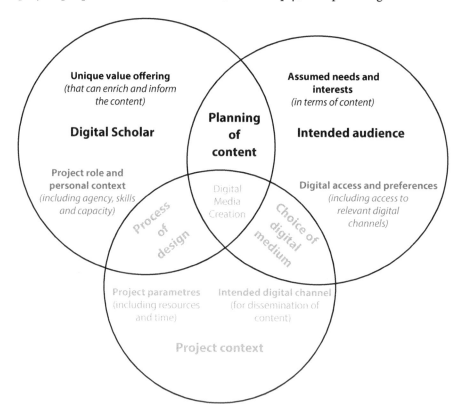

Figure 4.2: 'Planning of Content' – One of three phases in digital content creation

In order to unpack this part of the framework in more detail, one can consider the various dimensions of what the creator (i.e., digital scholar) can offer, and what their audience's needs are:

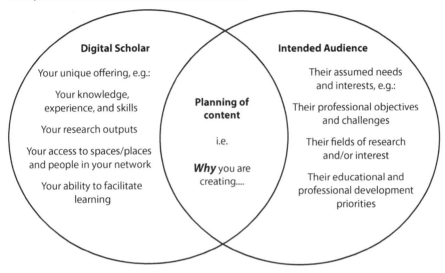

Figure 4.3: Planning of Content: The nexus between what the creator can offer and audience needs

Of course, truly 'knowing' an audience is hardly possible since the number of people that can be reached through virtual, online media channels is infinitely vast. A well-designed digital resource should therefore convey content in a truly captivating way, enabling the audience to retain the message, independently of the creator's digital or physical presence. The challenge, of course, is planning content for the rather unfamiliar, mostly virtual audience that will eventually engage with it. So, the first step for prospective 'creators' is to start with the more knowable variable, which is themselves.

Reflecting on the message you want to deliver
An awareness of the digital scholar's own capabilities and knowledge is key to their content development strategy. This does not mean they are not able or open to drawing on other people's knowledge (which is a capability in itself). Examples may include, but are not limited to, the following attributes:
- ✓ An in-depth understanding of a disciplinary field, and a resulting capability to digitally curate data, research outputs and multimedia.[24]
- ✓ Access to rare artefacts, interesting spaces (such as laboratories, restricted natural conservations or historical sites) and people (such

as industry experts, partners and colleagues) that others may have fewer opportunities to engage with.
✓ Knowledge and reflections, based on practical participation in research activities, service-related experiences and teaching activities.
✓ The scholar's own cultural, historical and social context, which may enrich the perspectives or assumptions of others (Dezuanni, 2015).

Considering what an audience will intellectually and emotionally respond to
Once you have taken stock of what you (and, potentially, your collaborators) contribute to the project, the next step is to consider the audience. Robinson (2019) makes the interesting argument that an 'audience' is different from how we imagine 'readership', as the former suggests the provocation of an emotional response or a spark of real interest (as opposed to just passive observation). So, it is essential for any effective communicator first to check their own assumptions about who is 'listening' before deciding what to say and how to say it (Veletsianos and Shaw, 2018).

For instance, the creator of a digital resource may want to consider whether the intended audience would benefit from firstly understanding the purpose of the material and message before engaging with the content (Xie et al., 2018). Perhaps they will better retain the message if the creator draws explicit correlations between the audience's expected lived reality and the message information being shared. If it is assumed that the message may provoke or induce scepticism, more case studies and relatable examples could be included. Or, if the creator wants to enable the audience to change their behaviour for the better, s/he may want to combine content that will trigger some form of an emotional response, followed by pragmatic suggestions to take action.

4.3.2 Choice of ICT and digital media genre
Going through the process of conceptualising content would have guided the creator to reflect on how their own experiences, skills or knowledge uniquely positions them to shape a message that could benefit a particular group of people. Deciding on the medium requires considering this presumed group of people through a specific contextual lens. The conceptualising of content is based on the anticipation of how the audience will engage with information on an emotional or intellectual level, whereas the choice of digital medium is primarily based on their physical environment and technical capabilities, i.e., *how* they will access the message.

The second contextual lens also relates to the project. Digital multimedia development mostly involves a project-based approach, resulting in an output that will be disseminated, potentially augmented and reapplied in multiple, unforeseen ways (Caldini, 2016). The practical parameters and opportunities within the 'project context' dictate how such delivery and dissemination will take place:

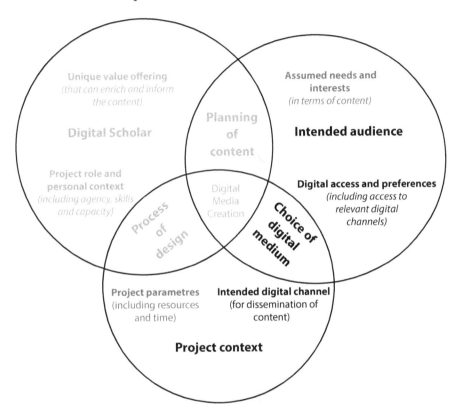

Figure 4.4: 'Choice of digital medium' – One of three phases in digital content creation

In order to unpack this part of the framework in more detail one can consider the various dimensions of the project context (i.e., how the content can be shared, given the project objectives and resources) and the intended audience (i.e. how it can access the relevant digital channels or platforms).

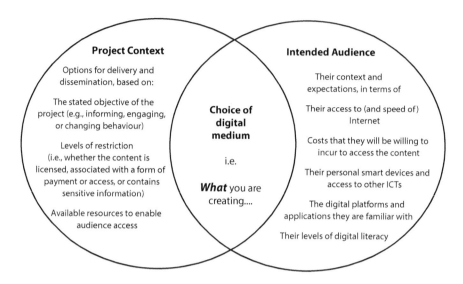

Project Context

Options for delivery and dissemination, based on:

The stated objective of the project (e.g., informing, engaging, or changing behaviour)

Levels of restriction (i.e., whether the content is licensed, associated with a form of payment or access, or contains sensitive information)

Available resources to enable audience access

Choice of digital medium

i.e.

What you are creating....

Intended Audience

Their context and expectations, in terms of

Their access to (and speed of) Internet

Costs that they will be willing to incur to access the content

Their personal smart devices and access to other ICTs

The digital platforms and applications they are familiar with

Their levels of digital literacy

Figure 4.5: Choice of Digital Medium – The nexus between the possible mediums the project parameters allow for, and the audience's context (in terms of reach, usability and access).

An **informal, personal or individual project** may allow for a digital file to be shared on any web-based platform of the creator's choosing – from a dedicated virtual classroom space to a personal blog, podcast channel, or simply a cloud-based link sent directly to selected individuals. The project context, in such a case, is quite flexible – the dissemination channel and intended audience are governed by the individual scholar. Scholars whose research takes them to various parts of the world may opt for setting up a podcast channel to capture and share audio interviews or soundscapes from their research-related travels. Others may wish to craft a more structured output such as a personal website that can feature a multitude of self-created resources – using tools that the creator is familiar with.

In other cases, a **broader project context** may be at play: The digital output may be created as part of a teaching mandate or funded research project, which would inform the choice of digital channel or platform for dissemination (e.g., an LMS, institutional website or affiliate blog), and therefore the appropriate media that can be uploaded and shared on that particular platform. In such cases, other variables should be considered: these may include quality standards (e.g., the base quality level for a video file to ensure consistency across project outputs), visual branding guidelines (e.g., the use of logos that signal which organisations or funders are involved), choice of communication channel (e.g., the choice between a blog or a project website), copyright considerations (i.e. the appropriate use of third-party material) and even the choice of language.

Project directives affecting the choice and application of media may sound inhibiting, but being able to draw on the resources of a bigger project can be creatively empowering: well-funded and larger scale projects tend to involve more technical support and offer wider reach. Creating video material, for instance, can be done on a small scale using entry-level editing software,[25] and – if the project is not representative of a larger initiative – the developer(s) should have more creative freedom to dictate the visual style and choice of content. For example, a larger project involving the development of video material could offer a larger budget, which typically allows one to draw on the specialist services of professional videographers and video editors. There are always drawbacks to complex projects, however, and the video development process may be subject to more structured processes (e.g., multiple rounds of scripting and storyboarding the narrative, obtaining location permits or talent release forms for presenters and actors).

Finally, all creative projects could benefit from a pre-scheduled **phase of evaluation and possible updates for improvement**. Ideally, this should be an iterative process, but the number of improvement cycles will also be subject to the project context: some formal projects may include a predetermined reporting phase on how various digital outputs have been applied and what the intended audience's response was.[26] In such cases, it would be useful to choose a medium that can be shared on a platform that incorporates some user analytics – such as anonymised activity reports on an LMS, or a podcast channel that can track so-called 'shares' and user engagement. Individuals may be interested in tools that will notify them if their infographic has been re-applied in other contexts or whether their podcast has reached members in their scientific community.

Of course, even if the chosen media genre is well-aligned with both the project brief and the creator's context, the end goal remains engaging the **audience.** How does this engagement take place? Every person that processes new information through digital resources does so through a physical action: seeing, hearing, touching or – in the case of immersive simulation – even smelling or tasting. It is an embodied activity, involving some kind of an engagement between our senses and a tangible technology. It is also situated in space (whether a virtual, Internet-enabled space or a physical space) and in time (whether it allows for dispersed, self-paced engagements, or whether it requires the audience's full attention for a specific period).

So – keeping the particular project context in mind – the choice of medium would be informed by a number of audience-related assumptions: Firstly, the use of ICT – despite the hyperconnected and globalised nature of our modern-day society – is still very much affected by the place occupied by its users. So, if it is expected that the audience will access the digital resources from a particular **geographic location**, this would affect the choice of digital medium: electronic access is improving all over the world, but there remains a large variability in the speed of Wi-Fi connectivity, and therefore varied opportunities for people from different regions to download large media files (Kanyengo, 2009). If the project is intended to reach rural areas or an audience that will find Internet data expensive, creating a large multimedia file that has to be downloaded or buffered online would not be ideal. Rather, longer videos can be edited into shorter clips, or compressed to smaller file sizes (if the type of content allows for lower visual quality). An audio or video podcast can be supplemented with a text transcript or summary. If the audience is expected to have only intermittent Internet access, choosing media that can easily be downloaded and stored on personal devices, for offline engagement at a later stage, is preferable.

Further, both the choice of media and the platform or channel where it will be shared should allow for equitable access (Reyna, Hanham, and Meier, 2018; Selwyn, 2014). The media creator will have to make a (preferably well-informed) guess about the **personal devices and ICTs** the audience would be able to access and their expected level of **digital literacy**. When assuming that the audience would not necessarily be well-acquainted with the relevant digital platform or channel, it becomes essential to subtly guide them on its optimal use: it cannot be assumed that younger generations – such as university students – are a homogenous group of so-called 'digital natives' that need no assistance to technically use and critically engage with emerging ICTs (Reyna, Hanham, and Meier, 2018). To ease the audience's engagement with a digital output one can provide user-friendly guiding prompts, such as a brief audio introduction or short video overview that demonstrates the intended use of the digital resource. Even a simple, text-based guideline could – for most digital resources of any media genre – equip an audience to understand not only the intended purpose of the project, but the intended application of the chosen technology.

Finally, every audience member will have to invest **time** to engage with a new digital resource: They will need to commit a sufficient and convenient period of time to watching, viewing, listening or otherwise engaging with the digital object. An audio podcast, for instance, allows the audience to conveniently listen to an episode while commuting (which would explain the increasing popularity of audio podcasts). Sometimes, a visually rich or interactive infographic may be preferable to written text, simply due to how quickly visual media can convey information (Moura, Almeida, and Geerts, 2016). If the intention is to command attention or evoke an emotional response within a short time period, a video clip or visual imagery may be a more suitable media genre for a broad audience than a purely text-based resource.

4.3.3 Process of design

The practical phase of the creative process (*how* to create) should ideally be preceded by the previous two phases that prompt the D.S. to carefully contemplate the intended content (*why* to create) and the appropriate tools, channel and medium for dissemination (*what* to create). The final design and development phase involves a commitment to practically exploring new tools and approaches, yet to remain cognisant of the project objective and infrastructure. This phase should be aligned to the creator's context as well as project mandate and structure (which typically includes a timeline, a budget, fellow collaborators and administrative requirements, amongst others):

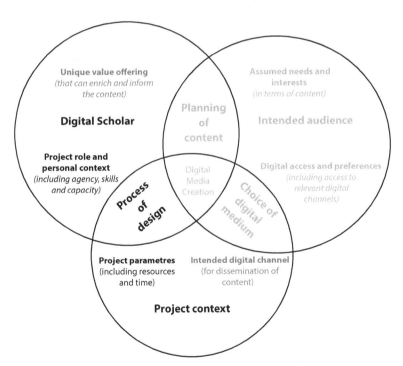

Figure 4.6: 'Process of Design' – One of three phases in digital content creation.

In order to unpack this part of the framework in more detail, one can consider the capabilities, role and personal context of the Creator (i.e., digital scholar), and how this aligns with the project context that includes practical parameters such as time, funding and shared objectives.

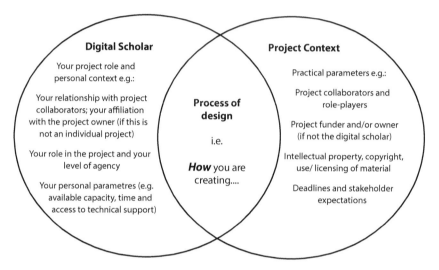

Figure 4.7: Process of design. The nexus between the creator's role and capabilities, and the project parameters

At this complex interface between the project infrastructure and the realities of the individual 'creator', there are a number of design process factors to consider:

The process of creating digital outputs tends not to occur in isolation:
The ability to foster productive collaboration can be a determining factor in successful digital multimedia creation. Each project requires technical support and guidance. The key is to find these support mechanisms as early on as possible. For institutional projects (e.g., related to one's role as lecturer or researcher at a university), it is worth enquiring about institutional software licences for multimedia creation. Colleagues in your immediate organisational unit, such as an academic department, can refer you to support staff members whose roles involve technical or professional development support. Alternatively, you can set up an appointment with a line manager or human resources representative for an exploratory conversation about the support systems available to you. Even individual projects can benefit from drawing on the expertise of more technically skilled collaborators to

help identify the appropriate editing software to use, or to provide critical feedback on visual design ideas.

The complexity of collaborating with others on a creative, cross-disciplinary project can be both challenging and immensely enriching. For larger-scale projects, multiple conversations and even disagreements may occur about which media genre to use, how to fix technical glitches and even how to determine authorship of digital material (Sayers, 2018). As this type of creative collaboration may be new to some, it is useful to have an open discussion about how labour will be organised and who has agency over which part of the creative process (Kaltenbrunner, 2015). It these joint efforts are approached symbiotically, there could be a digital output that exceeds any individual collaborator's expectation or area of individual expertise (Anderson and McPherson, 2011).

Creation involves innovation, but also mundane and unexpected tasks
Following on the previous point, the practical task of digital media development involves tasks that are administrative and technical. To sort and structure media files or to learn how to use a new graphic design software can at first seem menial, yet these tasks are part of the digital creator's role. Digital media creators will inevitably have the opportunity to control their content message, but they also have to play the role of technician and publisher (Brown, 2011). Fortunately, once a digital artefact has been created and shared online, it can be re-applied in multiple contexts without active participation from the creator. It may be necessary to update the content or style at a later stage, but this time investment should be minor in comparison to the first round of creation.

Basic digital media literacy is key, but can be incrementally developed through creative practice
The technical learning curve involved in digital media creation is accompanied by a deepened understanding of digital media principles, which, in turn, tends to improve scholars' generalisable communication practices (Parker, 2013). Some of these principles stem from graphic design practices. Research on visual media design bears testament to the importance of contrast between key text and supplementary content, the repetition of visual elements, the use of alignment and layout to indicate hierarchies and visual connections, and the use of proximity (grouping elements together) to indicate relationships (Williams, 2014).

Fortunately, developing digital media literacy does not require an academic understanding of multimedia. It can be honed through observation, practice and even intuition. A knowledge of media design principles and an awareness of empirical research on the subject is useful in other ways, such as equipping one to motivate creative design choices to collaborators (Kimball, 2013) whilst expanding one's own creative capacity (Mayer, 2006).

It can be helpful, for instance, to remain aware of how a clean visual layout, devoid of distracting elements and confusing patterns, improves engagement with online web pages, posters, animations and videos (Reyna, Hanham, and Meier, 2018). For a project that demands persuasion or a call to action, it is helpful to be aware how images can potentially carry more argumentative weight than text, even though visual elements tend to compound information more than detailed text (Rieder and Röhle, 2012). When generating a digital text-based resource, it is Röhle, to be equipped with a basic understanding of how a virtual audience engages with online text. A non-academic audience, for example, may respond better to text-heavy information that has been visually arranged around themes, that is succinct, and that strikes the appropriate level of conversational tone not to alienate the reader (Carroll, 2014).

Creation may involve curation

It should be acknowledged that the practice of creation is not limited to developing new outputs from the ground up. A key component of creation is selecting and re-arranging the building blocks already generated by others. Multimedia curation is a necessary skill in the digital age. It is essential to be able to responsibly and respectfully draw from others' creations in order to (co-)generate new understandings of our world.

Issues to be considered, in terms of digital media curation, include the need to stay abreast of copyright guidelines, legislation on the augmentation of existing digital artefacts, processes for obtaining permission to use third-party material, and 'borrowing' ideas from other groups and/or cultural groups. These considerations are important, even when working with 'open source material'. The vignette below showcases an excellent example of how digital curation can be, in itself, a practice of scholarly 'creation'.

Vignette: The scholarly practice of digital curation

At Stellenbosch University, South Africa, Magda Barnard is both an academic developer and a doctoral student. At the university's largest faculty (Economic and Management Sciences) she is responsible for programme renewal – a large and complex portfolio that requires her to switch her focus between very diverse contexts each working day. She has to stay abreast of emerging research in the field of curriculum studies, whilst responding to the practical queries and professional development needs of academic staff. A large portion of her work relates to quickly and effectively sharing information. For instance, she may have to apply pedagogical theories and concepts in one meeting, only to respond to a practical question around programme registration and accreditation in the next.

Fortunately, Magda has never shied away from exploring the affordances of digital tools at her disposal. Her rule of 'keeping it simple' has always served her well when she comes across, for instance, a new video-capturing software or online mind-mapping tool. As such, she has gradually started to record herself explaining key concepts or demonstrating the use of teaching tools by using freely available software such as 'Loom'[27] or 'Miro'.[28] Over the past five years, she has started building a rich multimedia repository of resources, ranging from 1-minute video and audio clips to infographics and digital mind-maps.

When asked why she thinks these resources are so effective and well-liked in the faculty, she explains that she creates them with an acute awareness of her audience's needs. She knows that the academic staff she works with are often in managerial roles. They need guidance quickly, but they also want to be able to return to more complex information sets in their own time and at their own pace. Her brief explainer videos are stored in an accessible cloud space where colleagues can re-watch them any time. Similarly, her visually engaging infographics and mind-maps are shared via links, so that she can update the content as required. She is aware that her environment is ever-changing, and so she always chooses online visual design software (e.g., Easel.ly[29]) that allows the user to return and update their cloud-based drafts at any time. Being able to draw from her repository of resources is saving her time in her professional practice, but it has also become a source of valuable data for critical reflection and research. She sees these digital creations as the artefacts that reflect how both her professional portfolio and the needs of academics in her faculty are evolving.

4.4   The way forward

✓ Try to maintain a curious mindset in terms of multimedia creation. Not only will new digital tools continually become available, but software you may already be familiar with will either evolve or be replaced. This calls for becoming comfortable with the discomfort of continually learning new skills and testing new solutions.

✓ Consider the various digital tools, platforms, software packages and applications available to you. Of these, consider which can best enable you to communicate your research, teaching or other scholarly work. If you are unfamiliar with any of the tools you consider applying, look for a collaborator with more technical expertise, so that you can learn with them, through practice.

✓ For your next project, conduct a context analysis, using the three-tiered framework, above. Before you start creating, consider whether you understand your audience's needs and context, your own capabilities and objectives, and your project parameters.

✓ Maintain realistic expectations. The creative process will not be an enjoyable one if you set an unachievable standard, in terms of how refined and complex your final product is. Your focus should be enabling, educating and ultimately serving your audience, as opposed to entertaining them (although appreciation and enjoyment could be a welcome outcome!).

4.5   Conclusion

We hope that this chapter has provided you with the realisation that creating digital artefacts forms an integral part of the journey of the evolving digital scholar. It is something we have all engaged in, by creating daily snippets of digital material – audio, video and visual – as means of capturing information and sharing knowledge.

To start any creative project in a scholarly context, the framework in this chapter should provide three possible starting points: an awareness of your own context (i.e., your skills, unique value offering), the project context (i.e., practical constraints and available channels for dissemination) and, most importantly, your intended audience (i.e., their needs, interests and digital access). Reflecting on each of these contexts should allow you to plan your content, help you to choose the most appropriate digital medium and plan your design process.

As you hone your digital creative skills, we trust that you will recognise the value of such a practical process that resides more in the act of creating, the lessons we learn from it, and the reflexive thought it generates than in the end results themselves. Deliberately choosing to adopt the position of 'creator' is a rewarding venture that allows us to learn how digital media can better enable the circulation of scholarship to a broader audience. In the next chapter we will reflect on how multimedia can be integrated and applied into different contexts.

References

Anderson, Steve, and Tara McPherson. (2011). "Engaging Digital Scholarship: Thoughts on Evaluating Multimedia Scholarship." *Profession* 2011(1): 136–51.

Brown, Susan. (2011). "Don't Mind the Gap: Evolving Digital Modes of Scholarly Production across the Digital-Humanities Divide." In *In The Culture of the Humanities*, ed. Daniel Coleman and Smaro Kamboureli. Edmonton: University of Alberta Press, 203-231.

Carroll, B. (2014). *Writing and Editing for Digital Media*. London, UK: Routledge.

Champion, Erik Malcolm. 2016. "Digital Humanities Is Text Heavy, Visualization Light, and Simulation Poor." *Digital Scholarship in the Humanities* 32(November 2016): fqw053.

Dallas, Costis. 2016. "Digital Curation beyond the 'Wild Frontier': A Pragmatic Approach." *Archival Science* 16(4): 421–57.

Dezuanni, Michael. (2015). "The Building Blocks of Digital Media Literacy: Socio-Material Participation and the Production of Media Knowledge." *Journal of Curriculum Studies* 47(3): 416–39. http://dx.doi.org/10.1080/00220272.2014.966152.

Kaltenbrunner, Wolfgang. (2015). "Scholarly Labour and Digital Collaboration in Literary Studies." *Social Epistemology* 29(2): 207–33. http://dx.doi.org/10.1080/02691728.2014.90 7834.

Kanyengo, Christine Wamunyima. (2009). "Managing Digital Information Resources in Africa: Preserving the Integrity of Scholarship." *International Information and Library Review* 41(1): 34–43. http://dx.doi.org/10.1016/j.iilr.2008.08.003.

Kellerman, David. (March 8, 2021). "Academics aren't content creators, and it's regressive to make them so". Times Higher Education. https://www.timeshighereducation.com/ opinion/academics-arent-content-creators-and-its-regressive-make-them-so. Accessed 27 May 2021.

Kim, S., S. Yi, and E. Cho. (2013). "Production of a Science Documentary and Its Usefulness in Teaching the Nature of Science: Indirect Experience of How Science Works." *Science and Education, Springer* 23(5): 1197–1216.

Kimball, Miles. (2013). "Visual Design Principles: An Empirical Study of Design Lore." *Journal of Technical Writing and Communication* 43(1): 3–41.

Mark E. Deschaine, PhD, and PhD Sue Ann Sharma. (2015). "The Five Cs of Digital Curation: Supporting Twenty-First-Century Teaching and Learning." *InSight: A Journal of Scholarly Teaching* 10(1): 19–24.

Mayer, R. E. (2006). Coping with complexity in multimedia learning (pp. 129-139). Elsevier Ltd., Netherlands.

Moura, Marlene, Pedro Almeida, and David Geerts. (2016). "A Video Is Worth a Million Words? Comparing a Documentary with a Scientific Paper to Communicate Design Research." *Procedia Computer Science* 100: 747–54.

Parker, JK. (2013). "Critical Literacy and the Ethical Responsibilities of Student Media Production." *Journal of Adolescent & Adult Literacy* (56): 668–676.

Reyna, Jorge, Jose Hanham, and Peter Meier. 2018. "The Internet Explosion, Digital Media Principles and Implications to Communicate Effectively in the Digital Space." *E-Learning and Digital Media* 15(1): 36–52.

Rieder, Bernhard, and Theo Röhle. (2012). "Digital Methods: Five Challenges." *Understanding Digital Humanities*: 67–84.

Robinson, James G. (2019). "The Audience in the Mind's Eye: How Journalists Imagine Their Readers." https://www.cjr.org/tow_center_reports/how-journalists-imagine-their-readers.php#_ftnref199.

Sayers, Jentery. (2018). The Routledge Companion to Media Studies and Digital Humanities *The Routledge Companion to Media Studies and Digital Humanities*.

Selwyn, Neil. 2014. Distrusting Educational Technology: Critical Questions for Changing Times. New York, NY: Routledge.

Sloman, S., and P Fernbach. (2018). The Knowledge Illusion: Why We Never Think Alone. Penguin.

Veletsianos, George, and Ashley Shaw. (2018). "Scholars in an Increasingly Open and Digital World: Imagined Audiences and Their Impact on Scholars' Online Participation." *Learning, Media and Technology* 43(1): 17–30.

Williams, R. (2014). The Non-Designer's Design Book: Design and Topographic Principles for the Visual Novice. Berkeley, CA: Pearson Education.

Xie, Kui, Gennaro Di Tosto, Sheng Bo Chen, and Vanessa W. Vongkulluksn. (2018). "A Systematic Review of Design and Technology Components of Educational Digital Resources." *Computers and Education* 127(April): 90–106. https://doi.org/10.1016/j.compedu.2018.08.011.

5

The Digital Scholar as Integrator: Why, how and where to bring your teaching, research and social impact to life

JP Bosman

This chapter focusses on

- ✓ Understanding the digital aspects and implication surrounding the practice of academic multimedia integration.
- ✓ The importance of cumulative knowledge-building, universal design for learning, open access and being critical.
- ✓ Useful digital curriculum and pedagogical design strategies, frameworks and planners.
- ✓ The creation of meaningful and persuasive multimedia resources.
- ✓ Pointers to how to design for and teach online.
- ✓ Potential digital platforms on which EDSs can perform their transformative integration 'magic'.

Keywords: Integration; cumulative knowledge building; Universal Design for Learning; Open Access; critical digital pedagogy; curriculum design; learning design; multimedia theory; digital platforms; online teaching.

5.1   Introduction

If an 'integrator' is someone who 'integrates', meaning to "form, coordinate, or blend into a functioning and unified whole",[30] then the evolving digital scholar (EDS) as integrator signifies the practice of skilfully combining separate textual and multimedia elements into powerful vehicles for cumulative academic knowledge-building. One could say that this skill, art or technique is becoming critical as part of the digital fluency of higher education practitioners. By technique is meant the "unnatural approach to a problem that, with practice, becomes second-nature. Technique is the non-obvious solution that amateurs and hard-working beginners rarely stumble upon on their own" (Godin, 2021). In higher education language the above points to the foundational frameworks, pedagogies and theories that are critical in seeing above the fray of the often very confusing and economically hyped-up world of digital technologies for learning, research and social impact. Let's explore the techniques of integration in the creation of valuable, high quality digital resources for teaching, research and social impact.

The Evolving Digital Scholar as Integrator designs, develops and curates multimedia artefacts to convey a message, i.e., with the intention to help the audience really to engage with and learn from it. The message (the story) is creatively and meaningfully designed and mostly packaged in a multimedia product and disseminated more openly with specific groups of people in mind, so that they can extend and apply it into their own contexts. Next to the tools to produce multimedia artefacts, the digital scholar also makes use of channels or instruments for distributing her/his work. These channels or platforms could include, but are not limited to, learning management systems (LMS[31]), personal or course websites, webinars, open-source repositories and possibly even teaching on a MOOC (Massive Open Online Course). In this chapter we explore the practice of "why", "how", and "where" evolving digital scholars can integrate their scholarly work in terms of teaching, research and social impact.

Apart from an introduction to techniques and digital platforms, the evolving digital scholar will discover some foundational theoretical insights into the world of designing for learning (in the digital world), and will learn to ask "to what end?" we are integrating as well as developing a necessary critical stance towards the digital world in which we are practising higher education. Since digital technology is changing by the day, an important reminder is that the practice of the digital scholar is evermore evolving. This asks for a certain digital fluency in which one is not trying to learn individual technologies one-by-one, but rather how digital technologies might function in support of our teaching, research and social impact service towards our institutions and society.

Although the journey of the evolving digital scholar is not necessarily linear (i.e., start with words (Author), then get comfortable with audio (Storyteller), then video (Creator) and then finally start integrating (Integrator)), there is something exciting about the practice of integration. This is because integration usually implies that you are building something of academic value and beauty which has the potential to transform the lives of students, higher education and society. You put something 'together' in a certain way on a digital platform so as to persuade, enlighten and educate. In this way integration is possibly at the heart of the digital scholarly practice. To achieve this persuasive enlightenment means that you should start reflecting on your own practice and understand how others can benefit from your scholarly output through the process of identifying and considering the needs of your audience. Integration also speaks to the ability to develop technical skills as well as the underlying principles/mindset required from you in this digital age. As mentioned in the previous chapter, it encourages you to 'learn to learn' continually – not just as a scholar but also as a digital citizen.

The pertinent digital skills in this section include, but are not limited to, designing blended, hybrid and online courses, by utilising digital platforms and educational applications that focus on visual presentation towards the building of powerful integrated multimedia mediated academic knowledge.

In order to unpack this part of the practice of being a digital scholar we are first going to take a theoretical step back and ask "Why?" or "To what end?" are we integrating. Then we will explore "How?" we integrate by looking at theory-informed frameworks, tools and approaches. Finally, we will end the journey by asking "Where?" our educational artefacts of integration can be built and shared.

5.2   Why or to what end do we integrate?

The field of educational technology in higher education has some potential blind spots which have been pointed out in recent research. We will address a general blindness to knowledge, a lack of design for universal access, lip service to open educational resources and practices and an uncritical adoption of digital technology. We will describe and address these tensions by suggesting a focus on powerful cumulative knowledge-building through semantic waving, developing Universal Design for Learning strategies, committing (even just a little bit) to working towards Open Access (OA), and fine-tuning our ability to have a critical perspective when it comes to teaching with technology. In doing this we highlight some of the bigger goals and ideas around our practices as evolving digital scholars.

5.2.1 *Integrate towards powerful cumulative knowledge-building*

We first take a look at knowledge itself as the important (often) "missing piece" of the educational/pedagogical puzzle because of a trend among scholars to feel overly comfortable in trusting in the "generic processes of learning" as well as often only focussing on the "knowing" part of knowledge (Howard & Maton 2011, p.103), thereby "obscuring the forms undertaken by knowledge practices mediated or enabled by technology" (Maton, Carvallo, & Dong 2016, p.77). These trends then create a culture among practitioners and especially instructional designers to focus more on the "technical matters" of design. Consequently, the "knowledge practices" or the *what* that needs to be learned often falls by the wayside (Maton et al., 2016 p.77). These actions can be described as a kind of blindness to knowledge (Maton et al., 2016 p.77).

The current mainstream thinking around using technology in education is to focus on learning design (with learning designers), which mostly builds on socio-cultural (social-constructivist) notions of pedagogy, as opposed to more traditional instructional design (with instructional designers), which has a positivist underpinning and a focus on multimedia (Conole, 2013). Even though there is a lot of merit in both these approaches (as will be discussed below), a particular focus on knowledge practices in blended, hybrid, active and fully online learning could be very beneficial for the future design and/or integration of educational resources into more powerful and cumulative knowledge-building strategies. But what is powerful cumulative knowledge, and how does one "build" it?

Knowledge is powerful when it is not segmented but cumulative. Segmented learning is typically either 'stuck' at the highly contextual instances of something to be learned (e.g., a lot of dislocated facts about many different things) or dwells only in the highly abstract/ 'theoretical' world of concepts. The problem is that the knowledge often does not 'travel' from the everyday to the specialised or the other way around (Hugo, 2013). Knowledge is powerful when it creates the "capacity for ideas or skills to extend and integrate existing ideas or skills" (Maton, 2014 p.1) or, in other words, it is about the "essential attribute" of the "recontextualization of knowledge" over time (i.e., cumulative) (Maton, 2013 p.20). To build this kind of knowledge (i.e., to develop your curriculum and pedagogy) one needs to understand the technique of semantic waving (Maton, 2013) or climbing up and down a "spiral ladder" which is a combination of the "transcendent" path into the esoteric abstract and the "immanent" path which "works from inside the everyday and finds in it everything that is needed to educate" (Hugo, 2013 p.28).

Semantic waving indicates that the focus is on the meanings of things (semantics) and that a visualisation of this kind of teaching and learning looks like a wave (waving). Through recent research into this phenomenon using the Legitimation Code Theory (LCT)[32] toolkit it is shown that teachers often use downwards or upwards "escalators" in their teaching practice (*Fig. 5.1*). They either teach by always starting with the concept/ theory/ abstract meaning (i.e., far removed from the context of the everyday) and then going "down" into the everyday world context by giving specific examples of the phenomenon that is learned. Then the next concept is again addressed at the abstract level, and then "applied" again by giving (practical) examples of how it works in specific circumstances. It can also be the other way around, i.e., always start with a practical example and then show what the theory is behind the example (moving "up"). The problem is that these practices often create segmented learning of knowledges that are in silos and students find it very hard (maybe even impossible) to "make the connection" between the different highly condensed meanings and how they relate to each other in the specific field of specialisation. This confusion then leads to the dreaded fear of memorisation for the exam only, with what is learned forgotten as soon as the ink has dried on the exam paper. Knowledge-building (learning) often does not happen because sense- and meaning-making do not happen, as the meaning was not "placed" in a "larger framework and context that holds elements together in a coherent whole" (Hugo, 2013 p.18).

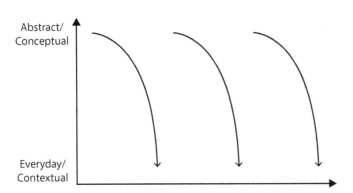

Figure 5.1: Example of teaching with "Downward escalators" in a segmented learning approach (Figure adapted from the heuristic figure in Clarence (2016)).

Semantic waving, on the other hand, can be visualised as a more continuous movement up and down between the specialised and the everyday, between theory and application, between the example and the concept:

> "whatever the field, the recontextualization of knowledge – an essential attribute of building knowledge over time – requires both upward shifts from specific contexts and meanings, and downward shifts from generalized and highly condensed meanings. Simply put, semantic waves represent the pulses of knowledge-building" (Maton, 2013 p.20).

A fairly simplified, but useful, approach would be to build one's curriculum, lesson, lecture, video, multimedia resource etc. according to semantic waves (*Fig. 5.2*). You can start (high) by introducing a new abstract concept (generalised and highly condensed), then (moving downwards) "unpack" the different meanings until you are (low) focussing on specific contexts and meanings. From there you then "repack" the meanings until you again integrate the knowledge at the highly condensed level, which then becomes the "platform" for building the knowledge to an even higher level. In so doing we see how "'powerful knowledge' comprises not one kind of knowledge but rather mastery of how different knowledges are brought together and changed through semantic waving and weaving" (Maton, 2014 p.1).

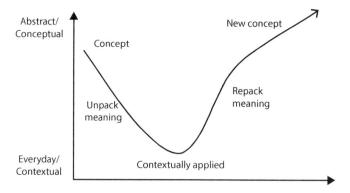

Figure 5.2: Teaching in a cumulative knowledge-building "Semantic wave" (Figure adapted the example in Maton (2014)).

The idea of cumulative knowledge-building through semantic waving (Maton) and of the interplay between the everyday and the specialised (Hugo) resonates with the idea of engagement, which is what lies at the heart of the potential for digital technologies in higher education. In the words of Oblinger (2014, p.14):

> "Many new learning environments foster student engagement that transcends memorization, immersing students in problem solving, collaboration, and active exploration and allowing them to construct, share, and transfer knowledge, not just recall it … Immersive learning experiences … move beyond 'teaching information' to helping students develop the valuable skill of 'transfer' – being able to take what they know and apply it to a new area".

The focus on students (or any audience, like other researchers or the public) brings us to the important question of how accessible "what" we integrate is. We have already seen how powerful knowledge can be made more cumulative by a focus on knowledge and semantic waving and weaving. Now we turn to a second, broader goal we should keep in mind in our practice as digital scholars, namely universal design for learning.

5.2.2 *Integrate with the aim of digital access for all – Universal Design for Learning*[33]

In a now almost iconic cartoon drawing the heartfelt reality of a non-universal access to a school is depicted. A student in a wheelchair is asking a person shovelling snow to please clean the wheelchair ramp, whereupon the person replies that all the other kids are waiting to use the stairs and that he will first clean the stairs and then clean the ramp. The response from the disabled student is piercing: "But if you shovel the ramp, we can all get in!" The spirit of universal access and universal design is captured poignantly in this cartoon, the basic premise being that if one creates accessible buildings and access to learning for people with disabilities, one is creating a system that is of value to all, both disabled and not. Michael Giangreco, the originator of the cartoon, captions it with the clear message: "Clearing a path for people with special needs clears a path for everyone!" (Giangreco, 2015 p.3).

Case study: A personal experience of print disability

"I recently had laser eye surgery and could not see properly for a good three weeks. To read on my cell phone and computer screen I had to all of a sudden turn to the assistive technologies available like screen readers, zoom text, and text highlighters. It was a very steep learning curve and made me very uncomfortable and tired. It also gave me a first-hand glimpse of what it must be like to suffer from a visual disorder, or a print disability.

After that episode I will never not think of how the texts I produce, the videos I make, the audio I record will be experienced by readers, viewers and listeners with various forms and levels of disability. Once you feel it in your heart it makes thinking about and taking action around Universal Design for Learning (UD4L) principles more of a reality." The chapter author, JP Bosman

In this section we look at how we can make our digital practice more aligned to UD4L. The mantra of the UD4L movement[34]/approach (CAST, 2018) can be summarised as follows:

✓ *Provide multiple means of **engagement***: The "why" of learning is addressed by multiple affective and flexible options for engagement in the form of interesting, stimulating learning experiences.

✓ *Provide multiple means of **representation***: The "how" of learning is supported with the teacher providing learning materials in different media and by giving lots of examples.

✓ *Provide multiple means of **action and expression:*** The "what" of learning focus points towards multiple and flexible opportunities for action and expression with the student practising differentiated tasks and demonstrating their learning in a diversity of ways.

These core principles emerged from CAST's research work on the neurological basis of learning, in combination with its practical work with learners (Dalton, Mckenzie, & Kahonde, 2012). Digital tools enable the teacher to design their teaching towards achieving these principles, but it can soon become complex and also create problems of its own. The fact that academics in higher education are able to create text, video and audio and integrate it into meaningful learning experiences through easy-to-use software and then instantly make it available through an institutional LMS or other platform can cause difficulties for students with special needs. Many academics do not even know about this crucial approach to creating and disseminating knowledge-building resources in a digital format and the few basic principles that can be followed by everyone to make a big difference.

Digital Practices around UD4L[35]

There are four main categories of disabilities, namely hearing, sight, motor and cognitive disabilities (Shekerev, 2019), and it is especially in the *sight disabilities* category that many of the digitally mediated problems occur. One can also address some aspects of dyslexia (a cognitive disability) under the vision-impaired category.

For *hearing disabilities* providing transcripts and subtitles with full captioning when video is used can really help, together with making sure the audio is of a high quality without any distracting background noises (Shekerev, 2019).

For *visual disabilities* like low vision, one should focus on the readability of digital texts, and for colour blindness one should steer away from green and red – although the reality is more complex – and rather work towards creating contrast between words and the background (Shekerev, 2019; World Blind Union, 2007). Of course, for blindness and more serious conditions like tunnel- or peripheral vision and macular degeneration, one needs to create resources and presentations that have an audio option (for video), and certainly for anything that needs to be seen and read on screen (like words and images) one needs to make it assistive technology friendly. This means that screen readers and devices like braille screen-readers must be able to "read" what is on the screen in a logical and clear way, and that images and other non-textual elements must be described using alternative text coding.

The World Wide Web Consortium (W3C, n.d.) provides very useful guidelines to make a start when one needs to understand how to change our web-based academic practices to being more universally designed for learning. The best is to focus on the basics,[36] which include:

(a) Always give images text alternatives (so-called "alt text") and make them meaningful and descriptive of the message the image wants to convey (e.g., if the image shows one how to plug a charger into a phone one should not provide the Alt-text as "Phone with charger" but rather "how to insert the charger into a phone").

(b) Use marked-up headings (e.g., Title, Heading 1, Normal etc.) with a logical hierarchical structure with the headings and labels clearly describing the topic or purpose. This includes making the page compatible with assistive technologies by simplifying the information architecture of your text/website/course and keeping the content clear and concise. And if you make a hyperlink, make the link text meaningful by, e.g., describing the content of the link target.

(c) Around readability, visual contrast (also called contrast ratio/ colour contrast) is key. This includes using clean sans-serif fonts (like Arial) and using text on solid backgrounds (i.e., stay away from background images). Text should also be able to get larger without overlapping other text in the process and one should never need to scroll horizontally to read sentences. There also should be as little moving, blinking or flashing content as possible, and when there is, the user should be able to control it.

(d) Multimedia (video and audio) elements should have alternatives like an audio file (for a video, preferably with more in-depth audio description) and transcripts and subtitles with full captioning for a video.

(e) Practically one can choose tools and platforms that have accessibility built into them (like WordPress, or Google-powered simple websites and blogging platforms) and when you want to inform yourself more there are free and open courses available.[37] It is also advisable to test your website/course/document for accessibility.

These basics are not only for web-developers to take note of (although developers have to go much further into the detailed and coding-oriented guidelines), but need to be taken seriously by the higher education evolving digital scholar as well. All these basics are within the reach and capabilities of academics. What is more, the prominent software- and operating system providers like Adobe, Apple and Microsoft[38] have gone to great lengths over the last couple of years to make their products accessibility friendly. This includes powerful built-in assistive technologies in major operating systems like Windows 10+ and Apple iOS, as well as accessibility checking tools for popular communication-, writing-, presentation- and universal document format software packages.[39] Also, the current LMS systems, like Moodle, Canvas and Blackboard, all have a strong focus on accessibility with supporting tools to move closer and closer to a UD4L offer for all its users.

There really is no longer any reason for anyone to say, 'I did not know (how).'

5.2.3 *Be open to being open*

In Martin Weller's (open access) book, *The digital scholar,* it soon becomes clear that the important sub-text is that digital scholarship goes hand-in-hand with an open and networked oriented approach to higher education (Weller, 2011). He describes openness as both a technical (like, e.g., open-source software and open standards) and a state of mind (the practice of sharing as a default) phenomenon (Weller, 2011). This commitment to openness is again confirmed in his important book, *The battle for open,* where he states that openness lies at the heart of the changes in higher education and that open educational practices are no longer seen as peripheral but accepted as more mainstream (Weller, 2014).

The call to openness in teaching usually gets bundled under the concepts of open access (when it comes to library and information science and publishing), open educational resources (OERs) and open educational practices (OEPs) (when it comes to teaching) and open data approaches (when it comes to research). The interesting thing is that it is now common for big research grants to include the prerequisite that the data collected be published in the open and often that the outcomes of the research be mediated and disseminated in the form of OERs or even (free) Massive Open Online Courses (MOOCs).

OERs are open access (often peer-reviewed) textbooks, documents, presentations, courses and other multimedia resources like images, audio and video. The development of the Creative Commons Licensing system[40] has made it possible to share an open resource in a nuanced and author-controlled way and indicates the different allowances that are provided for use. There are very useful global repositories[41] where one can publish or archive, and of course search for and access, a plethora of these different documents and media for use in courses, publications and research.

Open educational practices (OEP) are broader and "include the creation, use and reuse of OER, open pedagogies, and open sharing of teaching practices" (Cronin, 2017, p.15; see also Cronin & McLaren, 2018). These practices often include the opening up of policies as well as the development of student agency as life-long learners. The Cape Town Open Education Declaration (2007) takes the concept further:

> "open education is not limited to just open educational resources. It also draws upon open technologies that facilitate collaborative, flexible learning and the open sharing of teaching practices that empower educators to benefit from the best ideas of their colleagues. It may also grow to include new approaches to assessment, accreditation and collaborative learning."

Taking a Massive Open Online Course or being part of the development of a MOOC might just be the best thing you or your institution could do![42] It takes one far out of one's comfort zone, but it could contribute to tremendous accelerated digital learning opportunities for the individual scholar and can prove to be a kind of incubation space for an institution. At our institution (Stellenbosch University) the process of creating our own MOOC led to more institutionally focussed strategic thinking around the future of our own academic programmes, and as such led to deeper "organisational learning, resilience, and sustainability" as well as to the professional learning of participating staff members (Van der Merwe, Bosman, & De Klerk, 2020 p.175).

The idea of working in the open towards supporting open educational and research practices is difficult for some scholars as they sometimes struggle with their identity as sharing and networked scholars on the one hand and possibly being in a traditional university and department which frowns upon such practices and, therefore, are fearful of negative future career implications on the other hand (Weller, 2014). It also makes one potentially vulnerable to unfair criticism and attack as opposed to healthy critical scholarly debate. In this sense the vulnerability is akin to using social networking to promote your open educational and research practices, which is addressed in the next chapter where we deal with the scholar as networker. One must weigh up the advantages but, in a sense, also the direction in which higher education is moving (teaching and publishing) that pulls one to the side of the open. It is also important to understand that one has a digital 'shadow' on the internet anyway and might want to wrestle some control back by growing one's own digital 'footprint' (Goodier & Czerniewicz, 2015).

The development of open scholarship is intrinsically entwined with the development and use of digital technologies, and this is where we need to be careful not to be overly positive and enthusiastic. Which brings us to our final "to what end?" deliberation, namely, a healthy dose of suspicion.

5.2.4 *Always be critical – as a good scholar should*

Openness and the use of digital educational technologies are not without their baggage, and the evolving digital scholar should develop a healthy academically informed scepticism for when the next 'silver bullet' for solving all higher education's problems comes flying past, fired from the new OPM[43] 'sheriff' in town's powerful 'six-shooter'.

This is confirmed by Veletsianos and Kimmons when they press for a "critical examination of open scholarly practices, because the dominant educational technology narratives embraced in the field present an overwhelmingly positive picture of technology use in education that we believe is detrimental to our future" (Veletsianos & Kimmons, 2012, p.174). But the foundational fault lines run even deeper.

Laura Czerniewicz writes about the problem of digitalisation in Higher Education as being a sub-set of the extractive technology-based business models of broader society and that we are unable as yet to "provide robust alternatives as we are still in the early stages of imagining, researching and testing what these might be" (Czerniewicz, 2021). She points to the "grand experiment" of HE during the Covid-19 Pandemic and how profits have shot through the roof as proof of the marketisation of HE and what she calls "algorithmic academia" and "academic capitalism" (Czerniewicz, 2021).

This phenomenon is built on data extraction and surveillance capitalism strategies, not necessarily of personal data but rather on, e.g., the ambient student data (the "data exhaust") and the considerable risks when these data "become [...] consolidated into broader digital economic ecosystems" (Czerniewicz, 2021). Through more attentiveness to these new forms of coloniality, HE should resist this often rose-tinted future as sold by big tech and OPM companies, especially in times of crisis and vulnerability.

Apart from these broader issues, one must also identify how digital technologies can influence curriculum and an equitable student experience itself. Digital technologies often contribute to the hidden curriculum, which Edwards and Fenwick describe as "the things that are learned by students that are not intended outcomes of curriculum and pedagogy" and then goes on to explain that "the hidden curriculum is one of the primary educational ways through which social inequality is reproduced. The workings of the digital within such processes is of great significance" (Edwards & Fenwick, 2017 p.61). We should not see digital technologies as simply innocent tools through which we can do educational good (only), but also be sensitive to the fact that by choosing a technology we are already influencing what is taught and how it is taught. Their call to action is to be aware of these technologies' limitations as well as possibilities and that both lecturers and students should "examine their digital activity more critically" (Edwards & Fenwick, 2017 p.61).

This is not always easy, because the allure of a new educational tool or systems or approach is often so overwhelming that all caution is thrown to the wind as the teaching and learning "endorphins" rush through your brain while unboxing the 'new-and-shiny' or entering your credit card number for access to (almost) magical teaching tools.

With the "Why? Or "To what end?" questions sufficiently addressed, we can now move to things more practical as we first ask "How?" we integrate, and then "Where?" it can happen.

5.3 How do we integrate? Theory-informed practices around Integration

In a sense some of the "Why?" approaches above already are also "How?" integrating strategies, especially if we think of the creation of cumulative knowledge-building artefacts or courses through, for instance, using the semantic waving technique. The "How?" techniques are chosen because they are theory-informed and therefore can potentially be trusted more.

But it must also be said that we are now entering the world of curriculum, multimedia and learning design, which are all whole fields of knowledge in their own right. Whatever we do here will only scratch the surfaces of these practices and domains. The point of this section is not that lecturers become multimedia or learning designers, but rather to share some of the basic practices one can introduce in your own projects. We therefore turn firstly to the world of curriculum and learning design, and then to multimedia design and what it means to teach online.

5.3.1 Integrate with a plan – Curriculum and pedagogical design strategies, frameworks and planners

In curriculum development the old adage, "If you fail to plan you are planning to fail", rings true. Add the use of digital technologies to support your teaching and planning becomes critically important. Planning in higher education is usually done by using certain curriculum design processes that are built on particular frameworks which are in turn informed by a particular view of how learning happens.

Curriculum development- and design frameworks
At Stellenbosch University (South Africa), the professional home to three authors of this book, the institutional approach to curriculum or programme renewal is shaped by a typical educational design process and is informed by a learning-centred view of teaching and learning, and is fused to the very established technique of constructive alignment where curriculum objectives, teaching and learning activities (TLAs) and assessment tasks are aligned to create a system where all "components in the system address the same agenda and support each other" (Biggs, 2012 p.45). The students are "entrapped" in this web of consistency, optimising the likelihood that they will engage the appropriate learning activities" (Biggs, 2012 p.45). It is called the **D**esigning Learning, **T**eaching and **A**ssessment (**DeLTA**) framework/process[44] and guides departments and individual lecturers through different important aspects of curriculum and pedagogy design, namely: curriculum context, Outcomes, Assessments, Design for learning and Reflection (Figure 5.3). DeLTA is of course the mathematical symbol for change and therefore represents the outcome of following the process leading to transformative teaching and learning change at our institution (Stellenbosch University Centre for Teaching and Learning, 2020).

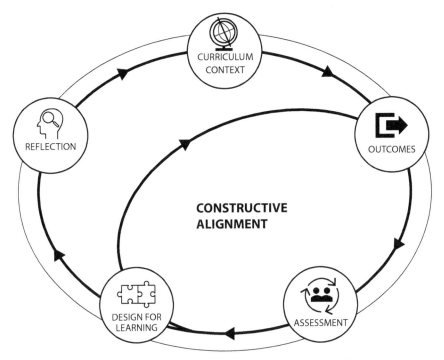

Figure 5.3: The DeLTA curriculum design process (Source: Centre for Teaching and Learning, Stellenbosch University).

Other well-known design frameworks that are proven to help one think through the broader design of one's course or programme (or any educational project) is ADDIE (Analyse, Design, Develop, Implement, Evaluate), (which still is) a favourite of learning designers, various Design Thinking processes and the Carpe Diem process of Gilly Salmon. But often what is needed when one wants to start to use digital technologies for one's teaching are techniques that help one design meaningful blended or online teaching and learning activities.

Diana Laurillard's brilliant book, *Teaching as design science: Building pedagogical patterns for learning and technology,* and the Conversational model that highlights the six (6) types of learning provide powerful thinking tools for designing your course, and at our institution (SU) we have been using it with great success (Laurillard, 2012). University College London's ABC Learning Design toolkit[45] is based on Laurillard's theory and can be of great help to the evolving digital integrator.

Gilly Salmon's[46] e-tivities concept is also a wonderful structuring tool for creating active learning activities in online courses. Any e-tivity you design is based on an action-response principle and is aimed at getting every student actively to engage with a "spark" you provide (often in the form of a controversial or very informative reading or video). It starts with crafting the invitation (including the important spark) to the e-tivity and then goes through phases of individual response and then a collaborative dialogue.

Digital curriculum development tools
The digital scholar does not have to look far to find digital tools to help with the planning and design of curriculum or learning activities. Gráinne Conole provides the convincing rationale for her excellent "round-up" digital visualisation and pedagogical planner tools (Conole, 2013, p.97):

> "...teachers are bewildered by the plethora of tools available and the lack of skills necessary to make informed learning design decisions. Therefore, a key facet of all the tools is that they attempt to provide practitioners with some form of guidance and support around their design practice. The aim is to help them shift from an implicit, belief-based approach to design to one that is more explicit and design-based."

Under *Visualisation tools*[47] she reviews the LAMS, WebCollage, CADMOS and CompendiumLD systems. Under *Pedagogical planners*[48] she looks at DialogPlus, Phoebe and The Learning Designer (Conole, 2013). At our institution we resonate with the Learning Designer as it is underpinned by Laurillard's Conversational framework and can help the practitioner build lessons and courses that are rich in learning potential and overtly incorporates technologies as well as other educational "favourites" such as formulating meaningful learning outcomes, Bloom's Taxonomy, and indicating time-on-task, among others. The Learning Designer can be accessed at http://learningdesigner.org – try it out, it works!

5.3.2 *Making cognitively pleasing and persuasive multimedia resources*
Once one has properly designed for the learning, the next step is to create resources or, more than that, start to build integrated educational resources or experiences. Inadvertently in this digital age one will turn to the combination of words/text, images, audio and video in a meaningful and cumulative knowledge-building experience. Sometimes one has funding and can outsource the whole process to teams of experts. Sometimes one can get help from a team or an individual in a support role at one's institution. But

often you (or you and your team) have to just jump in and get your hands dirty. It helps (a little) to have some multimedia design tricks up your teaching and learning sleeve.

In the previous chapter, the evolving digital scholar as Creator,[49] we have already dealt with this aspect and the reader is urged to study that part again.

5.3.3 Teaching collaboratively online (in emergencies) – some pointers

We would be amiss to not say anything about teaching online in emergencies, especially as this book was written in the terrible time of the Coronavirus Pandemic, starting in 2020. The whole educational world was turned upside down, and within the space of a few weeks teaching at our institution had to "pivot online". The approach was later named Emergency Remote Teaching (ERT), and even later Emergency Remote Teaching Learning and Assessment (ERTLA). Our colleagues in the Learning and Teaching Enhancement division at Stellenbosch University (Strydom, Herman, Adendorff, & De Klerk, 2020) compiled a book about an aspect of this experience and we quote extensively from the introduction:

"The onset of COVID-19 in South Africa came near the beginning of the academic year. Academics across South Africa were obliged to rethink their TLA offerings. Academics at Stellenbosch University (SU) were compelled to prepare for and institute emergency remote teaching (ERT) to replace conventional face-to-face (F2F) student interaction with fully online learning. It was communicated in the SU community that the purpose of ERT was not to create a robust online educational ecosystem. The aim, rather, was to establish a temporary online initiative that could be easily set up and provide opportunity for continuous, just-in-time support by responding to the evolving needs of students and teaching staff. Consequently, ERT required the rethinking and adaptation of our existing offering for delivery via SUNLearn, the university's Moodle-based learning management system (LMS). Our objective was to design for active student involvement and to encourage students to take responsibility for their own learning whilst keeping the approach as simple as possible" (Strydom, Herman, Adendorff, & De Klerk, 2020 p.2).

A new kind of liminal teaching and learning shadow world came into being, not being fully online (as there was not enough time and expertise in the staff complement), but not being able to just turn face-to-face into face-to-screen learning environments.

We quickly learned that our main approach should be asynchronous and not synchronous. This means more self-study and flexibly timed learning activities interspersed with opportunities for real-time contact between lecturers and students. It meant the recording of short, knowledge-distilled screencast video-lectures of core concepts. It meant creating (often for the first time) logical, simple and well-structured courses on the LMS. It implied constant and clear communication between the institution, faculties, departments, lecturers, professional academic support staff and students. It required asking radical questions like "Do I really need my students to write an exam?" and emergency adaptations to assessment strategies. It asked institutions and academics alike to listen to the student voice and respond as best possible to their unique fears, anxieties and needs. If students did not have a laptop the institution provided laptops. If the students did not have data for internet, the university provided data-bundles. Never before has the reality of the potential and the pitfalls of teaching and learning in the digital world been more starkly experienced by role players. Professional support and academic staff came together to collaborate and learn from each other. Academics worked collaboratively in departments and faculties to solve common problems and identify possible educational solutions. Students were brave beyond measure – the stories of academic resilience in the midst of great suffering making one humble.

These experiences were situated not only in conventional higher education settings. Some of the authors, for instance, became involved with the African University Network for Higher Education in Emergencies[50] in designing open access augmented webinars related to digital pedagogy in emergency educational environments.[51] Presenters quickly realised that what came as a shock to more traditional HE environments were 'normal' for displaced persons or refugees. By focussing on digital pedagogical strategies that can 'work' for refugee students, we are hoping to develop and co-create the type of knowledge that all HE institutions should be ultimately geared towards, namely a pedagogy that invites and accepts all learners and provides a flexible learning experience. In that sense it supports a Universal Design for Learning approach, but just on a very broad scale.

When we raise our gaze a little towards a more conventional online teaching practice, one of the most helpful frameworks for designing successful online courses is the Community of Inquiry (COI) model. We argue that even in emergency remote teaching environments this pedagogical approach has the potential to make a difference in students' successful learning journeys. Just having good (and even great) content online is not going to create an exciting learning experience for your students. For optimal engagement in an online course the COI "presences" should be strived for. The original description of CoI originated from Garrison, Anderson & Archer (1999): "The Community of Inquiry (CoI) is a theoretical framework for the optimal design of online learning environments to support critical thinking, critical inquiry and discourse among students and teachers".

The basic assumption is that the importance of social, cognitive and teaching presence in a course will lead to a COI focussed on knowledge building (Garrison, Anderson & Archer, 1999):

> *Social Presence.* The ability of participants to identify with the community, communicate purposefully in a trusting environment, and develop interpersonal relationships by way of projecting their individual personalities.
>
> *Cognitive Presence.* The extent to which learners are able to construct and confirm meaning through sustained reflection and discourse in a critical Community of Inquiry.
>
> *Teaching Presence.* The design, facilitation and direction of cognitive and social processes for the purpose of realising personally meaningful and educationally worthwhile learning outcomes.

It is, however, not only the individual realisation of the presences, but their interplay with each other, that adds the most value towards a transformative educational experience. Bektashi (2018) gives a very helpful overview of COI and how it supports the use of technology in learning. Volschenk et al. (Volschenk, Rootman-Le Grange, & Adendorff, 2020) draw on COI to underscore their view that successful teaching online is not about technology – it is about humanising:

> "Humanizing online learning is an effective and practical teaching strategy that at its core attempts to inculcate human interaction and an inclusive environment in online teaching … It is posited that through building engaging human relationships/interactions and fostering a sense of community and connectedness among students, effective and authentic learning takes place" (p.70).

The relationality of online pedagogy also extends to the people who 'create' the courses, and this brings us to our final insight. Teaching (and the design thereof) asks for a team approach. Gone are the days of 'going it alone'. For instance, Kahn (Kahn, 2017) argues:

"Teaching in higher education *is* a collective endeavour. It requires the commitment and agency of teachers, learners and others in order to be undertaken well. Excellent teaching is determined on a wider basis than simply the individual competence of lecturers" (p.168).

Because of the digitally connected nature of the world we live, teach and do research in, we can use that connectedness to change the culture of HE to one of open collaboration in support of a more just society.

Now that we know a little bit more of 'how' to integrate, we turn to the last piece of the puzzle: 'where' should we share, publish, advertise, and teach our products of integration?

5.4. "Where" to integrate?

Ninety per cent of the evolving digital scholar's integration projects will probably be on an institutional LMS or other learning platform that is accessible only by those institutions' students and lecturers. The challenge with a closed access system like this is that often the university's copyright and intellectual property policies make it quite difficult to follow the advice of "being open to being open". Learning Management Systems (or Virtual Learning Environments) have been with higher education for almost 25 years and have been associated with different overarching metaphors like 'straightjacket, behemoth, digital carpark, safe space, smorgasbord, path-finder and now (in the time of the Covid Pandemic) a limpet' (Farrelly, Costello, & Donlon, 2020):

> "The educational tide may rise and fall; political, economic or biologi-cal storms may lash the higher education sector, yet VLEs have shown a remarkable ability to adapt and ingrain themselves into the teaching and learning landscape. In fact, as educational providers have pivoted into a world of purely online delivery, VLEs have become the de facto campuses of the world" (p.7).

The challenge is to try and apply the foundations, frameworks and func-tionalities of curriculum, multimedia and learning design in a course in an institutional LMS. That being said, LMSs have matured and become fairly usable to the point that, with creativity and focus on the basics of blended and fully online learning, one can get quite far and create high quality and learning-centred courses.

For the other 10 per cent, there is a whole new world outside the LMS that awaits the brave academic digital traveller. Apart from social media, such as Facebook, WhatsApp and Twitter (which is often the more "open" or "revolting" choice of platform for lecturers who feel handicapped by (only being allowed to use) the LMS), there are emerging digital spaces and systems that allow you to integrate open access, universally designed, knowledge-building practices as needed.

Of course, there are too many options to list here, and they will date fairly quickly, so I will try and create a typology of sorts. Is the platform or service suitable for the institution or more for the academic as individual? And, then, is the platform more open-access, or more closed-access inclined?

The following table (*Table 5.1*) tries to give some ideas of types of platforms within this typology with some current examples to bring it down to current digital realities.

	Open Access possible	Closed access
Institution focus	MOOCS, micro-credential type courses and programmes * www.edx.org * www.futurelearn.com * www.getsmarter.com Unstructured, more flexible course delivery platforms: * https://drive.google.com * www.edmodo.com * https://ed.ted.com	Learning Management Systems (LMS) * www.moodle.org * www.blackboard.com * www.instructure.com * https://classroom.google.com * https://teams.microsoft.com
Individual focus	Digital Portfolio platforms that allow lecturers (and students) to build personal- or professional learning portfolios: * www.bulbapp.com * https://sites.google.com Websites which offer a blog component for creating your own internet presence on your own terms: * www.wordpress.com * www.blogger.com * www.wix.com Course hosting sites for when you want to participate in OEP activities and share your knowledge freely (or for a small fee) outside your institution: * www.zillearn.com * https://www.p2pu.org/en/ OER knowledge repositories for when you want openly to license and share your (hard made) image, video, presentation, graph, infographic, notes or course: * www.wikipedia.org * https://www.oercommons.org/ * https://www.oerafrica.org/ * Your own institution's OER repository	Professional portfolios * www.linkedin.com * www.academia.edu MOOC-type or other paid for courses that are open to individual teachers to contribute to: * www.skillshare.com * www.udemy.com

Table 5.1: Typology of digital platforms as they relate to individual-institutional and open-closed perspectives.

5.5 Suggested way forward

✓ Think about how knowledge "works" in your specific discipline and try and map some of your "lessons", lectures or presentations using the concept of semantic waves. Are you surfing the wave, or are you riding downward escalators?

✓ Challenge yourself consistently to practise the UD4L digital basics, like alt-text, using heading styles, thinking about contrast etc., and in that way making a difference in all your students' academic lives.

✓ Be more critical when you read about the newest educational technology "silver bullet". See if you agree with the new tool's possible ethical or security implications. Become part of your institution's thinking around digital pedagogies and systems and bring your open or even difficult questions to the discussion.

✓ Think of starting an Open Access project in which you (or your students) publish something that can be used openly by anyone in the world. Remember to assign a Creative Commons Licence!

5.6 Some final integratory remarks

What about integration and research, or social impact? Well, one could say that all the knowledge and skills gained as an integrator in the teaching sphere of digital scholarship can also be transferred to the research and social impact domains. We have already discussed in Chapter 3 some strategies for science communication to the public through storytelling and audio, which can be enriched and expanded on to include more daring multimedia adventures.

And then there are gems to be discovered like Jove,[52] a platform for scientists to publish their science and laboratory methods in video format. The site has over 10,000 videos and more than 1,000 participating universities! Or OpenStax,[53] a non-profit organisation that publishes high-quality, peer-reviewed, openly licensed college textbooks that are absolutely free online and low cost in print.

Last but not least, remember your own institution's marketing and communication department, who can be an important ally in your quest to evolve your digital presence as a scholar!

References

Bektashi, L. (2018). Community of Inquiry Framework in Online Learning: Use of Technology. In R. Power (Ed.), *Technology and the Curriculum: Summer 2018*. Ontario: University of Ontario Institute of Technolgy.

Biggs, J. (2012). What the student does: Teaching for enhanced learning. *Higher Education Research and Development*, 31(1), 39–55. https://doi.org/10.1080/07294360.2012.642839

Burgstahler, S. (2015). *Universal Design in Higher Education : from Principles to Practice* (2nd ed.). Cambridge, Massachusetts: Harvard Education Press.

CAST. (2018). Universal Design for Learning Guidelines version 2.2. Retrieved January 9, 2021, from https://www.cast.org/impact/universal-design-for-learning-udl

Sherran, C. (2016). Surfing the waves of learning: enacting a Semantics analysis of teaching in a first-year Law course, *Higher Education Research & Development*, DOI: 10.1080/07294360.2016.1263831

Conole, G. (2013). Tools and resources to guide practice. In H. Beetham & R. Sharpe (Eds.), *Rethinking pedagogy for a digital age: Designing for 21st Century Learning* (2nd ed., pp. 78–101). New York: Routledge.

Cronin, C. (2017). Openness and praxis: Exploring the use of open educational practices in higher education. *International Review of Research in Open and Distance Learning*, 18(5), 15–34. https://doi.org/10.19173/irrodl.v18i5.3096

Cronin, C., & MacLaren, I. (2018). Conceptualising OEP: A review of theoretical and empirical literature in Open Educational Practices. *Open Praxis*, 10(2), 127. https://doi.org/10.5944/openpraxis.10.2.825

Czerniewicz, L. (2021). Coloniality, profit making and market expansion – the shape of the past and the future? Retrieved February 15, 2021, from https://czernie.weebly.com/blog/archives/01-2021

Dalton, E. M., Mckenzie, J. A., & Kahonde, C. (2012). The implementation of inclusive education in South Africa: Reflections arising from a workshop for teachers and therapists to introduce Universal Design for Learning. *African Journal of Disability*, 1(1). https://doi.org/10.4102/ajod.v1i1.13

Edwards, R., & Fenwick, T. (2017). Knowledge infrastructures, digital higher education and the hidden curriculum. In B. Leibowitz, V. Bozalek, & P. Kahn (Eds.), *Theorising learning to teach in higher education* (pp. 59–73). London: Routledge.

Farrelly, T., Costello, E., & Donlon, E. (2020). VLEs: A Metaphorical History from Sharks to Limpets. *Journal of Interactive Media in Education*, 2020(1), 1–10. https://doi.org/10.5334/jime.575

Giangreco, M. F. (2015). Crisscrossing from Classrooms to cartoons: Social science satire. *Counterpoints*, 463, 3–15.

Godin, S. (2021). Natural technique doesn't exist | Seth's Blog. Retrieved January 11, 2021, from https://seths.blog/2021/01/natural-technique-doesnt-exist/

Goodier, S., & Czerniewicz, L. (2015). Academics' online presence: A four-step guide to taking control of your visibility. *OpenUCT Guides*, 48. Retrieved from https://open.uct.ac.za/handle/11427/2652

Howard, S., & Maton, K. (2011). Theorising knowledge practices: a missing piece of the educational technology puzzle. *Research in Learning Technology, 19*(3), 191–206. https://doi.org/10.3402/rlt.v19i3.17109

Hugo, W. (2013). Cracking the code to educational analysis. Cape Town: Pearson.

Kahn, P. (2017). Teaching in higher education as a collective endeavour. In B. Leibowitz, V. Bozalek, & P. Kahn (Eds.), *Theorising learning to teach in higher education* (pp. 175–171). London: Routledge.

Laurillard, D. (2012). Teaching as design science: Building pedagogical patterns for learning and technology. New York: Routledge.

Maton, K. (2013). Making semantic waves: A key to cumulative knowledge-building. *Linguistics and Education, 24*(1), 8–22. https://doi.org/10.1016/j.linged.2012.11.005

Maton, K. (2014). Building powerful knowledge: The significance of semantic waves. In E. Rata & B. Barrett (Eds.), *The Future of Knowledge and the Curriculum*. London: Palgrave.

Maton, K., Carvallo, L., & Dong, A. (2016). LCT in praxis: Creating and e-learning environment for informal learning of principled knowledge. In K. Maton, S. Hood, & S. Shay (Eds.), *Knowledge-building: Educational studies in Legitimation Code Theory* (pp. 72–92). London: Routlegde.

Meyer, A., Rose, D. H., & Gordon, D. (2014). *Universal design for learning: Theory and practice*. Wakefield: CAST Professional Publishing.

Oblinger, D. G. (2014). Designed to engage. *Educause Review, 49*(5), 12–33.

Shekerev, N. (2019). Accessibility guidebook for web development. Retrieved January 27, 2021, from https://www.telerik.com/blogs/web-accessibility-guidebook-for-developers

Stellenbosch University Centre for Teaching and Learning. (2020). Designing Learning, Teaching and Assessment (DeLTA) process.

Strydom, S., Herman, N., Adendorff, H., & De Klerk, M. (Eds.). (2020). *Responding to the necessity for change: HE voices from the South during the COVID-19 crisis*. Stellenbosch: Stellenbosch University – Division for Learning and Teaching Enhancement. Retrieved from http://www.sun.ac.za/english/learning-teaching/ctl/Documents/Responding to the necessity for change.pdf

Van der Merwe, A., Bosman, J., & De Klerk, M. (2020). The development of MOOCs as incubation space for professional and institutional learning. In K. Zhang, C. J. Bonk, T. C. Reeves, & T. H. Reynolds (Eds.), *MOOCS and open education in the global south: Challenges, successes, and opportunities* (pp. 169–180). New York: Routledge.

Veletsianos, G., & Kimmons, R. (2012). Assumptions and challenges of open scholarship. *International Review of Research in Open and Distance Learning, 13*(4), 166–189. https://doi.org/10.19173/irrodl.v13i4.1313

Volschenk, H., Rootman-Le Grange, I., & Adendorff, H. (2020). Successful online learning and teaching is not about technology – it is about humanizing. In S. Strydom, N. Herman, H. Adendorff, & M. De Klerk (Eds.), *Responding to the necessity for change: Higher Education voices from the South during the COVID-19 crisis* (pp. 69–74). Stellenbosch: Stellenbosch University – Division for Learning and Teaching Enhancement.

W3C. (n.d.). Accessibility – W3C. Retrieved January 27, 2021, from https://www.w3.org/standards/webdesign/accessibility

Weller, M. (2011). The Digital Scholar: How technology is transforming scholarly practice. London: Bloomsbury Academic.

Weller, M. (2014). *The Battle for Open: How openness won and why it doesn't feel like victory.* London: Ubiquity Press. https://doi.org/http://dx.doi.org/10.5334/bam

World Blind Union. (2007). WBU PowerPoint Guidelines: Guidelines on how to make the use of PowerPoint and other visual presentations accessible to audience members who have a vision or print impairment. World Blind Union. Retrieved from https://www.ifla.org/publications/guidelines-created-by-the-world-blind-union-wbu-on-how-to-make-the-use-of-powerpoint-an

6
The Digital Scholar as Networker: Re-thinking why and how we 'network'

Miné de Klerk

In this chapter we focus on

✓ What a social network really entails, and how social network analysis can help us better understand the key features of social networks.

✓ The necessary shift in thinking about scholarly networking: from self-promotion (of the individual) to service (of a network's purpose).

✓ Practical networking tools for the digital age.

✓ Networking for teaching, scholarship and service.

Keywords: Professional networking; social networks; academic networking; social networking sites; academic conferences; virtual conferences.

6.1   Introduction: Considering networking and social networks

In the context of contemporary scholarship, the term 'networking' is typically associated with digital or in-person events that are explicitly organised to enable knowledge-sharing and expanded professional networks. Typically, such events – conferences, seminars or even workshops – allow those in attendance to inhabit the same place (or virtual space) at the same time, to allow for some form of social engagement and professional relationship-building. These professional acquaintances (or so-called 'connections') are expected to enable academic career advancement, to spark research collaborations, or even lead to future employment. Networking has, of course, extended to the asynchronous[54] virtual space, where a social media profile page is now the digital equivalent of a business card, allowing us at any moment in time to connect with a global network of individuals that can potentially serve our professional interests. Both in-person and online networking can further be supplemented with less intentional endeavours, involving more serendipitous, informal engagement that can eventually lead to professional relationship-building.

Wherever and however networking occurs, the reason scholars (or any other type of professionals) engage in career-related networking tends to be informed by their individual, vested interests. The Cambridge dictionary defines networking as "to meet people who might be useful to know, especially in your job",[55] whereas the Merriam Webster explains it as "the exchange of information or services among individuals, groups, or institutions. specifically: the cultivation of productive relationships for employment or business".[56] Based on these definitions and our common understanding of the term, *networking* involves the pursuit of new acquaintance and deepening of existing relationships as a means to serve professional objectives.

Such an understanding of networking as an activity primarily related to individual progression is somewhat at odds with our still evolving understanding of how complex social networks grow and sustain themselves. In order for an individual *to network*, one would assume their point of departure would be to understand the underlying goal of the social network they intend to participate in. This understanding aligns with research showing that our professional identity in academia is inextricably linked to an ever-evolving understanding of both the professional and social networks we occupy, and our sense of connection to our place within them (Heidari et al., 2020).

So, before delving into how scholars can best navigate social networks in an increasingly digital world, it is useful first to consider what constitutes a *social network*. One way to do this is to draw from social network analysis (SNA).[57] Neither a methodology nor a theory, SNA provides a useful perspective for better understanding the nature of the social systems that all humans form part of. The starting point of SNA is that our social lives are fundamentally subject to relations between individuals or groups (Marin & Wellman, 2016). Although this may seem a glaringly obvious premise, it does challenge many of our intuitive assumptions about our role in the social world. It highlights that we tend to infer causal relationships between the *individual attributes* of actors within a network (such as ourselves) and the *behaviour of the entire network.* For example, we may assume that one colleague's personal attributes (e.g., skills or knowledge) are somehow directly responsible for the achievements of a much larger social network they participate in. A structural perspective of social networks, however, shifts the focus from individual attributes to the *linkages between* individuals. These linkages – whether they are communication channels or personal relationships – are treated as the primary clues to understanding social behaviour, as opposed to studying the traits and skillsets of separate individuals (Freeman, 2004).

To illustrate how social networks can be understood, we can consider a hypothetical scenario:

Scenario: Illustration of how social networks can be understood

An innovative initiative was launched at a South African university. It involved a highly successful new mentorship programme that connected young researchers, seasoned scholars and industry leaders in their field. The initiative evolved into what was widely deemed a regional and later international success. It was shown to enable productive collaboration between emerging researchers and practitioners, whilst advancing the professional profile of the established scholars and mentors involved.

To understand why the scheme was so effective, one approach would be to investigate the characteristics and skills of selected individuals who played a critical role in mobilising the programme. Another approach could be to focus on the academic departments or administrative centres involved at the relevant universities.

A social network analyst decides to apply another approach in her investigation:

1.) **She focuses on *the links* between those involved** in the programme, e.g. the nature of their professional or personal relationships, and how information flowed between relevant individuals (Marin & Wellman, 2016).

2.) **She cautions not to limit her understanding of networks to encompass only easily identifiable groups** (such as departments, organisations or other groups that are typically defined by membership). Rather, she seeks to understand sub-networks in the programme that evolved more organically, around a shared purpose or common interest (Davis & Sumara, 2009).

Her approach leads her to identify a social network of well-acquainted scholars, spanning different academic departments. She finds that, in the early stages of the initiative, they actively shared their common interest in supporting the programme amongst one another. As a result, they played an essential, yet not apparently obvious role in the pilot phase, as they encouraged one another to reach out to private-sector contacts that eventually provided crucial funding sources to sustain the programme through its initial grassroots phase. They further offered informal mentoring to early-career scholars involved in the programme. Their unstructured network may be less easily identifiable than a dedicated team or well-established organisational unit, but the boundary-crossing nature of their network made it a key enabling factor in the establishment of the programme. The information they exchanged (as opposed to the sum of their individual parts in term of their traits and skills) allowed new opportunities to emerge.

To summarise, social networks are not necessarily limited to groups with clearly articulated agendas, formal titles or any form of membership. Rather, social networks emerge beyond and across the boundaries we tend to intuitively recognise. Fields such as SNA further suggest that these networks are products of human interactions – digital or otherwise – as opposed to an aggregation of a group of individuals. As such, the relationships between people within a network can tell us more about how the network will behave than the sum of their individual attributes could (Fetterman, 2014; Freeman, 2004; Marin & Wellman, 2016; Pierpaolo, 2011). Finally, social networks allow broader, more complex systems to evolve and sustain themselves – offering essential mechanisms for information exchange, often referred to as *feedback loops* (Koopmans, 2017; Mccool et al., 2015; Scott et al., 2018).

This perspective of social networks can serve to guide one's understanding of professional networking. The dictionary definitions of 'networking' signal the importance of information exchange, but they also suggest a stronger focus on the personal objectives of the individual, independent of the purpose of the social system they occupy. For the digital scholar, there certainly is much individual-level personal and professional reward to be gained from networking, as the rest of this chapter will outline. However, these benefits will always be the result of our ability to serve the underlying purposes of the social systems we navigate in the process. If the basis of networking is a genuine curiosity about others within the network, an openness to learn, to collaborate and to engage in dialogue, then the individual rewards associated with networking activities – such as academic career progression and research accolades – could follow as a result.

6.2   A shift in thinking about networking

As referred to throughout this book, digital scholarship is concerned with the exploration and application of emerging technologies to transform scholarly practices in an increasingly hyper-connected society (Jordan & Weller, 2018; Weller et al., 2013). This includes the ability to creatively apply digital tools (software, applications, smart devices and online platforms) to engage with social networks that will help to evolve their scholarly and/ or teaching praxis. Academic social networking sites (ASNS), for instance, have become more widely used by academics in recent years,[58] and it was initially expected that these platforms would lead to more active and wide-spread research collaborations (Jordan & Weller, 2017). Research has shown, however, that academics' motivations to engage in online networking are more related to promoting themselves professionally, promoting their own research outputs, searching for and accessing resources and advancing their careers (Jordan & Weller, 2018). Similarly, academic conferences – virtual or otherwise – tend to be approached more as a platform for self-promotion than for fostering collaboration (see the section on 'conferences', later in this chapter). This is not to say that self-promotion is problematic per se. In fact, the potential reach and visibility that digital networking tools allow is a valuable affordance in the context of academia:

> "In a world where academic faculty members are judged by the number of works that they publish and the number of citations that the works receive, an instrument that allows them to influence the extent of their exposure and increase the likelihood of citation delivers much power and utility" (Meishar-Tal & Pieterse, 2017, p. 17).

Exposure and influence are, of course, attractive benefits in this context. However, these gains are not automatically realised simply through using online networking tools. We know (as shown earlier in this chapter) that social networks evolve and grow as their members actively participate within them, with the goal of adding value to the broader network *before* expecting professional benefits to themselves. Veletsianos and Kimmons (2012) term such synergy between the individual scholar and their online networking tools and social practice as *networked participatory scholarship*.[59] It involves not only sharing professional profiles and research outputs online, but also reflecting upon, critiquing, validating and continually developing one's scholarship (Veletsianos & Kimmons, 2012). It can be argued that this participatory approach would add more value to the entire network as opposed to limiting the expected value-addition only to the individual. As earlier discussed, social networks evolve through dialogue and relationships, and we can safely assume that human relationship-building relies on participation, synergy and acts that lead to mutual gain.

So, let us consider the various motivations of professional networking in the context of scholarship, teaching and service in order to identify a more participatory approach to networking in the digital age.

6.2.1 Networking for scholarship
6.2.1.1 Academic Social Networking Sites

One of the most popular ways for academics to network online is the use of academic social-networking sites (ASNSs). Prominent examples include ResearchGate, Mendeley, Academia.edu., CiteULike, Penprofile, Bibsonomy, Zotera and Epernicus. These sites are designed in a similar way to more generic social networking sites, as they allow users to upload content and follow other users' profiles or communicate with them, but they are also more intentionally designed to meet the needs of scholars (Asmi & Madhusudhan, 2015). In addition to these common functionalities (which one would find on a social networking site such as Facebook, or a professional one such as LinkedIn), ASNSs typically include features such as citation count, altmetrics, reference management and collaborative document processing (Espinoza Vasquez & Caicedo Bastidas, 2015). Some of these sites, such as ResearchGate, CiteULike and Mendeley, also allow for users to create and share their own profiles, so that they can 'follow' other scholars with similar research interests and gain access to their related networks and their publications (Thelwall & Koucha, 2014).

Given the social features of these sites, one would expect a key drawing card for users would be the potential for interactions between individuals with mutual scholarly interests. However, researchers tend to use ASNSs mainly to consume information, to a lesser degree to share information and very rarely to interact with other site users (Meishar-Tal & Pieterse, 2017). Another key motivating factor at play when it comes to how ASNSs are used is the career stage of each individual subscriber. Seasoned academics tend to use online social networking sites primarily to raise the profile of their work in a research community, whilst junior academics and early-career researchers tend to be interested in ASNS to foster relationships that can lead to research collaboration in their field, or for future career prospects (Jordan & Weller, 2018).

Although these sites are continually integrating more social engagement functionalities, the platforms are still primarily used to upload articles and track citations (Ovadia, 2014). Fittingly, self-promotion, ego-bolstering and the acquisition of knowledge are shown to be the most enticing affordances for academics that make use of these sites (Meishar-Tal & Pieterse, 2017). As such, academic online platforms tend to be designed primarily to satisfy the scholarly community's needs for information-sharing, with social engagement as a secondary objective (Boyd & Ellison, 2007). These sites' discussion boards or direct-messaging capabilities may not be as visible or seamlessly integrated as one would find on a non-academic SME, such as Twitter or LinkedIn – platforms designed for communication and networking as a primary advantage. A number of ASNSs, such as Academia.edu and ResearchGate were intentionally developed to facilitate connection between users with profiles. A myriad of other platforms such as Mendeley were initially designed for sharing academic content, and social networking functionalities were added at a later stage (Jordan, 2019). Longer-time users of these academic sites may not have explored their more recent social networking capabilities simply because they have learned to use the platforms with their primary function, i.e., the dissemination of academic content, in mind.

The information-sharing function of ASNSs still remains a key networking affordance. As mentioned earlier, the starting point for productive networking should be the question: how can I add value to the broader network, in terms of a shared goal or common interest? ASNSs can circumvent the model of official academic publishing that – after a lengthy publishing timeline that can exceed a year (for refereed academic journals) – tends to limit access to online academic databases (Thelwall & Koucha, 2014). Most ASNSs allow authors to upload full texts of their published work, their conference presentations and even drafts for public consumption and comment.

In terms of online communication, however, it is fair to assume that scholars using ASNSs also have other social media accounts, and that they may find engaging in online discussions on all these platforms too time intensive. While scholars also appropriate non-academic SNSs such as Facebook and Twitter for professional purposes (Jordan & Weller, 2018), the challenge of time and capacity, especially for those balancing their research endeavours and a high teaching load, still remains. Using various SNSs for both professional and personal purposes, to disseminate and find resources but also actively to communicate with others, will invariably impact on any scholar's (assumingly already limited) capacity and time. At the end of this section we share suggestion on how this can be addressed.

6.2.1.2 Social Networking Sites[60]

Social networking sites (SNSs) that have not been designed for academic purposes, such as Twitter, Facebook and LinkedIn, are increasingly becoming part of the scholarly community's online networking toolset (Faucher, 2018; El-Shall, 2014). These social sites can be used as a complementary tool for academic SNSs – becoming a means for academics to establish professional relationships beyond their circle of social contacts. The very social design of these sites that focus more on profiles and people than on academic content allows scholars to gain insights into their field in the context of public discourse and the lived experiences of those outside academia. Even so, non-academic SNSs or related smart device applications are often regarded as trivial or even inappropriate by the scholarly community. Researchers in the field of complexity thinking have warned against this, arguing that without the capacity to constructively engage with social networks, scholars limit the impact of their work (Mccool et al., 2015):

> "By taking the time to understand who within a given network seems to be connected to everybody else, and investing in relationships with those individuals, we can not only learn considerable lessons about what the people they know think, we also have an increased opportunity to influence the system we are embedded within."(Mccool et al., 2015, p. 315)

For the digital scholar, the mix of professional and personal observations on SNSs can be a productive and highly effective approach to understanding their audience better. The informal and personal nature of engagement on these platforms can function as hooks for establishing connections with individuals relevant to their field, and can help scholars to better communicate their research to a broader public (Weller, 2011). The broader reach of these social platforms can also influence how the professional identity of the scholar is formed as they learn to understand the values, views and personal contexts of those beyond their academic circles, i.e. the rich mixture of practitioners and scholars from a range of fields which may benefit from their work (Heidari et al., 2020). In the digital humanities, for instance, scholars found Twitter to be an essential tool for raising awareness of trends in the field, and to invite insights from both scholarly peers and interested members of the public (Quan-Haase et al., 2015).

For scholars that want to focus on the emerging – perhaps still informal – discourses forming around their work and field, blogs pose a useful opportunity for open, yet structured online engagement. Academic blogs that welcome productive debate can help to establish scholars as public intellectuals, as they allow them to share and log their formal research outputs whilst the blog authors can share and welcome more personal (often light-hearted) reflections about the scholarly experience (Veletsianos & Kimmons, 2012).

The following table (Table 6.1) provides practical suggestions for using social networking sites for digital scholarship.

Academic SNSs
✓ **Subscribe and create a well-rounded profile** on a popular and well-established ASNS to gain access to a broader network of fellow scholars. Your online profile should include essential background on your professional expertise, discipline, interest for collaboration and, potentially, links to your institution and relevant social networking sites.
✓ **Consider your unique needs and whether they align with the site's affordances.** For example, research-related networking can be facilitated on ResearchGate.net, Academia.edu, OrcID, Publons and Scopus, whilst the popularity of Mendeley is largely due to its automated bibliography features. A quick Google search on 'best academic social networking sites' will lead to an array of useful blog posts or discussion forums summarising and comparing key features of prominent ASNSs. These typically include tools for impact measurement, citation tracking and other forms of aggregated data on how often content is viewed or downloaded. Be sure to look for more recent articles, as the functions of ASNSs continually evolve.
✓ **Keep in mind that establishing connections via these sites requires *adding value to the network*.** Regular information-sharing can spur productive dialogue and even collaboration with others. The resources you upload can range from published texts to conference papers and even drafts. For the latter, be sure to indicate clearly that they are in draft format, and update them once published.
✓ **Explore the communication mechanisms on the site**. Most of the sites allow users to update their profile settings so that they are alerted when other users comment on their uploads, so that they can reply. Another common, useful setting is the option to subscribe to a discussion forum.
✓ **Keep it simple. Discussion threads need not be long and online communication need not be time intensive.** A simple word of praise or thoughtful question on a peer's work can establish or deepen professional relationships. If you receive multiple questions or comments, it is also acceptable to post a single response that addresses some of the most useful questions and thanking others for their feedback.
Non-academic SNSs
✓ **Approach social media as a source of enjoyment, rather than a chore.** Although applications such as Hootsuite allow for pre-scheduling posts and managing content on various platforms, managing too many profiles can start to feel like a menial task. Approaching social media as a source of gratification and curiosity, rather than dedicating a set time to it each day or week, is shown to be more effective for academic users (Britton et al., 2019; Tsapali & Paes, 2018).
✓ **Remember that networking is a two-way street**. Your choice of social network site should be informed by i.) your professional needs, and ii.) what value you can add to social networks on the site. First consider the central function of the platform, and whether you can (or want to) contribute to it. For example, Twitter allows for quick dissemination of information, via re-tweets, link sharing and hashtags. It is actively used as a source of breaking news, and as a mechanism for spreading viral news, which involves news stories that reach a wider audience at a much more rapid pace than other news stories (Al Rawi, 2019). Other platforms such as Facebook allow for more blog-like posts and are popular for setting up and advertising centrally managed collaboration pages. This will be elaborated on later in this chapter. Career-focused platforms such as LinkedIn allow for recruitment opportunities and career-related achievements to be shared, with profiles set up to function as digital resumés.

✓ **Seek quality engagement above quantity of 'likes' or 'shares'.** The size of your network should be a secondary objective, whilst high-quality information exchange and productive engagement should be the primary goal. Choose a smaller number of channels (such as one ANS and one SNS for professional networking), where you can disseminate high-quality, thought-provoking content that aligns with your scholarly interests, but possibly also invites dialogue with others. Whilst SNSs are designed to provide you with quantitative metrics on engagement (e.g. the number of 'likes', 'shares' or followers), a large network is not necessarily a reflection of the value it can add to you, and vice versa (Mainka et al., 2015).

✓ **Find a balance between generating your own and sharing others' content.** This will simplify and sustain the information-sharing process. For sharing your own content, consider linking from the SNS (e.g., Twitter or LinkedIn) to the academic platform (e.g., ResearchGate), where you upload your research outputs or the blog where you engage in more in-depth discussions. When you re-post hyperlinks to interesting resources you find on the Internet, contextualise and enrich the posts by adding your own thoughts along with the link, and invite others to share their thoughts on it.

✓ **Practise online etiquette (often referred to as 'netiquette').** This includes giving credit to someone online – even if you are re-posting a direct link to their work – by either linking to their relevant online profile (e.g., 'Twitter handle') or their institutional contact page. In terms of online discussions, constructive disagreement can lead to valuable new insights, but engaging in public disagreements without practising sound netiquette carries a high risk. Online communication tends to be more visible and logged more permanently than in-person discussions (see below).

✓ **Remain cognisant of the risks associated with social media.** Social media accounts, whether for personal or professional use (or a mix of the two), are public and therefore always carry a reputational risk. Even posts on direct messages or private discussion boards can by law, in most countries, become the subject of your employer's scrutiny. Online discussions related to teaching material or research findings can also be shared out of context, or invite abusive comments from what are now commonly known as 'online trolls' (Britton et al., 2019). There is no single solution to these risks. It is advisable, however, to treat the virtual space as a transparent one, where one can expect at some stage to weather (and hopefully ignore or delete, as opposed to indulge in) bullying behaviour.

Table 6.1: Practical suggestions for using social networking sites for digital scholarship.

6.2.1.3 Conferences

Much has been written about the value of oral presentations of conference papers in terms of enriching and complementing the written research article. Presenters have the opportunity to relay their ideas in a more dynamic way by communicating with listeners through their physical gestures, facial expressions, variations in tone of voice, and (often) the use of multimedia to emphasise key points (Lynch, 2011). In addition to the opportunity to listen to the research presentations of their peers, face-to-face conference participants have multiple opportunities socially engage with their scholarly community. This typically include poster presentations, question-and-answer slots, roundtable discussions, social 'mixer' events and ICT-enabled 'backchannels' such as conference-specific Twitter accounts or hashtags (Brusilovsky et al., 2017). Despite the common perception that academic conferences are ideal networking hubs, research suggests that there are a number of issues inhibiting the potential for interpersonal engagement and rich dialogue at these in-person events. According to the extensive research conducted by Rowe (2018), these issues include (but are not limited to):

✓ the large scale and high-paced programme of these events, which inhibit small-group and personal interaction,
✓ a reliance on uni-directional podium presentations and limited plat-forms for audience interaction,
✓ place and time restrictions which lead to a high number of concurrent events, and
✓ limited or no access to information about presentations that delegates may have missed as a result of time and place restrictions.

The virtual conference model addresses some of these issues in apparent ways. Abstracts can be accessed online; presentation can be recorded and live-streamed (or replayed at a later stage) to a wider audience. Virtual sessions allow for larger group participation, and more diverse panel members can participate as they do not face travel restrictions (Lessing et al., 2020).

When the COVID-19 pandemic forced academic conferences to move online in 2020, the change in delivery mode was welcomed by sectors of the scientific community that, long before the global crisis struck, made the case for decarbonising conference travel. As commented in *Nature*, the sum of travel for all delegates to attend a single, large face-to-face academic conference can release as much CO_2 as an entire city would in a week (Klöwer et al., 2020). For many delegates that could not afford the travel costs associated with conference attendance, the 2020 shift to virtual conferences would also have been welcomed. A study analysing conference attendance numbers showed that higher education institution/scholarly society conferences incur annual costs of between 8.9 and 39.9 billion US Dollars, at the minimum level (Rowe, 2018). Delegates' international travel and high registration fees contribute significantly to this sum (Niner et al., 2020).

Given that digital scholarship is concerned with open information exchange, accessibility issues associated with in-person conferences should also be critically considered. Especially young researchers can be adversely affected by the in-person conference model, not only in terms of the personal or institutional costs involved, but by the networking challenges they experience during the conferences themselves. Without the guidance or facilitation of more established peers in the relevant academic community, young researchers tend to find it difficult to establish relationships with more seasoned scholars or potential collaborators at conferences (Camedda et al., 2017). A virtual conference model that offers higher and more equitable participation, along with environmental benefits, is therefore quite attractive. This does not mean there is no place for the in-person conference. The sense of scholarly community that emerges from sharing a physical space with peers, the richness of face-to-face communication (which allows for more nuanced cues conveyed by body language and tone of voice), the welcome informal engagement that can occur during intervals between presentations, and the sheer joy of travelling to interesting conference sites are certainly features that the virtual conference can hardly imitate. However, the virtual conference, seminar or workshop can also form an essential part of the digital scholar's networking toolkit. The following table (*Table 6.2*) gives some practical suggestions relating to virtual conferences or online events.

Attending or participating in virtual events (conferences, workshops or seminars)
Do (even more) preparation work beforehand. Whilst in-person events will allow you to network with peers in interim social spaces (e.g., during refreshment breaks), opportunities for interaction during virtual events tend to be subject to a more structured programme. To ensure that you do not miss the opportunity to engage, be sure to prepare questions around the topic. Text-based questions can even be pre-typed, to be copied and pasted in a chat forum.
Be intentional about expressing encouragement and thanks. As virtual events are devoid of cues of appreciation such as applause, speakers will likely welcome a word of thanks after their presentation – whether typed in a chat forum or sent as a brief email after the event.
Consider how you can best engage using text-based chat functions. Whereas you will not necessarily be required to use your webcam as a participant, text-based channels are a staple feature of online conferences, workshops and seminars (Levy et al., 2016; Niner et al., 2020). When other participants cannot see or hear you, the chat pane may be the only space to establish your presence. If you are allowed to post comments before formal proceedings start, consider treating the chat as a conference lobby where you greet the group and introduce yourself, or acknowledge a contact you know. Active engagement in small-group discussions can also serve to establish new connections, but be careful about the typical pitfalls of computer-mediated communication, such as domineering online discussion or interrupting others (Vandergriff, 2013). Try to build upon others' contributions, so that a generative 'thread' of inclusive, online dialogue can emerge.
Organising or facilitating online events
Think creatively about how to leverage the vast affordances of remote events. Rather than attempting to replicate the format of an in-person conference, list the affordances of the virtual model that align with your audience's needs (see below). Explore opportunities to invite more diverse panel members, emerging researchers, practitioners or even interested members of the public. Identify which expert/panel presentations can be pre-recorded and shared in advance to prepare the participants for discussion, and what would be best to present in a synchronous ('real time') modality.

Avoid applying the face-to-face event programme to a virtual event. Participants may not be willing to spend sustained periods of time passively viewing their computer or tablet screen. The temptation to multi-task is also larger when the participant is in front of their work device or at home. So, approach the event as a mix of online, offline, individual and group activities. A workshop can be facilitated as a number of short, focused sessions over a more extended period, interspersed by or preceded with pre-recorded videos, audio podcasts or text-based resources. Participants can then engage with activities in their own time in order to prepare for the live engagements. If a single, full day event is necessary, schedule sufficient breaks in between presentation slots, breakout group engagements (e.g., using Zoom or Microsoft Teams) and include moments for informal interactions near the start, middle and end. 'Ice breaker' exercises to socialise the group could be considered.

Before you start your planning, consider your audience's needs:

✓ *Identify a unique topic that will spark active engagement.* With the low financial barrier to organising an online conference there is no limit to the number (and variation in quality) of such events. To add value to your professional network, spend enough time investigating the niche focus or current relevancy of the event theme. Keep in mind that the purpose of synchronous online events is interactive engagement, not passive observation. Including topics that will invite debate or active contribution in small group discussions will lead to productive networking during the event.

✓ *Consider the participants' time zone.* If the participants will engage remotely from regions in different time zones, you will have to find a timeslot that will suit the majority, even if this falls outside their typical workday hours (Niner et al., 2020). For smaller groups you can send an online survey beforehand with options to vote for the most suitable timeslot. Before the event, ensure that those that cannot attend know where and when recorded resources will be disseminated.

✓ *Consider their Internet access.* The COVID-19 pandemic adversely affected the ability of scholarly communities in emerging countries to participate in virtual conferences. If a large portion of the audience does not have access to reliable, high-speed Internet, consider replacing online models with a hybrid programme, e.g., sending delegates pre-recorded video resources, followed by shorter online sessions with the option to engage with the presenters and delegates via asynchronous (self-paced), text-based discussion forums.

✓ *Plan the start (introduction) and the end ('next steps') carefully.* Choose the conference platform wisely. Consider your needs (e.g., live streaming to large groups via YouTube or other public platforms, managing Q&A and chat functions, and enabling breakout discussions). Videoconferencing platforms add new features regularly and can be challenging (for you and the participants) to stay abreast of new features. So, choose a platform that is freely accessible, widely used and that offers sufficient onboarding material (i.e., technical 'how to' guidelines for new users) that you can share with participants beforehand. Ensure your event programme includes active hyperlinks for quick navigation to the relevant virtual spaces, and ensure you have a colleague that can assist you during the event, in case you experience any technical difficulties yourself.

Table 6.2: Practical suggestions relating to virtual conferences or online events.

6.2.2 Networking for teaching

The positive correlation between online teaching communities and the professional development of teaching praxis is well recorded (Jordan & Weller, 2018; Veletsianos & Kimmons, 2012). Whereas online networking in the context of scholarship is more closely related to professional collaboration and career advancement, online networking activities related to teaching and learning are more related to information-seeking and skills development (Thelwall & Koucha, 2014). A survey of academics about how they use social networking tools related to teaching showed that digital networking spaces were primarily used as a teaching tool to facilitate and organise student learning.[61] To a lesser extent, SNSs and blogs were used to establish communities of practice and to discover new resources related to pedagogy (Gruzd et al., 2018).

The tendency for online professional networks to have a strong resource-sharing focus makes sense, given that teaching is a practical, often individual endeavour. Scholarly networking, as illustrated earlier in this chapter, is strongly focused on seeking research collaborations, career advancement opportunities and means to gain access to the most up-to-date research findings in a particular field. Teaching-related professional networks, on the other hand, also reflect a prominent need for advice from more experienced teachers, examples of how learning can be facilitated in a particular field and accessible teaching resources that can be reapplied in different contexts (Viskovic, 2006).

Social networks that develop around a shared interest in teaching often form in a departmental or institutional context. Colleagues that experience similar teaching challenges – often related to online learning – are shown to find each other's context-specific resources and reflections on relatable experiences an enabling factor in their professional development (Davis et al., 2019). In some cases, these social networks evolve into more organised teaching communities of practice (e.g., aimed at helping teachers to navigate policies, evolve their scholarly approach to teaching and seek formal mentorship), whilst other networks are more unstructured in nature, involving ad hoc information-sharing and informal social engagement as means of professional and emotional support (Baker-Doyle, 2011). In both cases, digital networking is proving an invaluable mechanism for establishing and sustaining teacher networks. Social communication platforms offer a sense of social connection and support that is less hindered by geographic boundaries. During the COVID-19 pandemic, for example, virtual coffee-breaks between fellow teachers became a popular mechanism for professional support (Pepe et al., 2020). Another powerful benefit of online teaching networks is the ease of sharing examples and tools with others. This practice of sharing and copying resources within human networks is shown to strengthen the network itself, by increasing the capacity of the people within it, and helping them to navigate the complexity they face (Mccool et al., 2015).

6.2.3 *Networking for service*

In the introduction to this chapter we considered the notions of social networks as phenomena best understood based on the nature and strength of the relationships between people. This perspective of professional networking allows us to shift our focus to mutually beneficial exchanges. This means any personal gains are welcome, yet indirect outcomes of our efforts to contribute to the system as a whole. To network, in this sense, is essentially an act of service to our community – professional, scholarly, or beyond.

Serving the purposes of a social network need not be costly in terms of time or finances. Consider which academics or public figures you follow online. You will note that the most interesting of these individuals are not displaying the type of 'networking' behaviour that suggest a primary concern with career progression or ego-bolstering. The literature tells us that these individuals are interested in social networks as platforms to ask questions of their peers, to draw from the expertise of a wider community, and – by following profiles or scholars they admire professionally – to determine what research to read (Jordan & Weller, 2018).

Given that digital scholarship is underpinned by a spirit of open collegiality and active engagement (Kaltenbrunner, 2015; Quan-Haase et al., 2015; Weller, 2011), responding to such needs in our social networks should be not only intuitive but also personally rewarding.

For example, consider how networking as a service can occur on various levels – from the small-team or departmental-level to the scale of global networks:

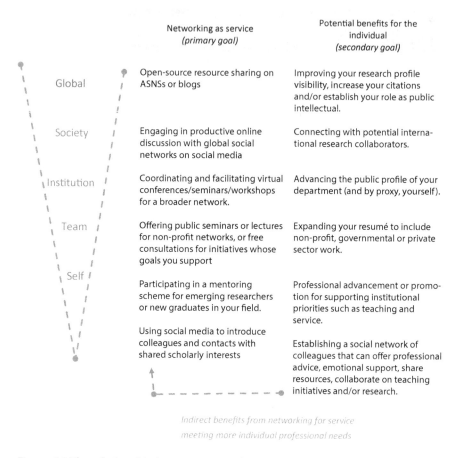

	Networking as service *(primary goal)*	Potential benefits for the individual *(secondary goal)*
Global	Open-source resource sharing on ASNSs or blogs	Improving your research profile visibility, increase your citations and/or establish your role as public intellectual.
Society	Engaging in productive online discussion with global social networks on social media	Connecting with potential international research collaborators.
Institution	Coordinating and facilitating virtual conferences/seminars/workshops for a broader network.	Advancing the public profile of your department (and by proxy, yourself).
Team	Offering public seminars or lectures for non-profit networks, or free consultations for initiatives whose goals you support	Expanding your resumé to include non-profit, governmental or private sector work.
Self	Participating in a mentoring scheme for emerging researchers or new graduates in your field.	Professional advancement or promotion for supporting institutional priorities such as teaching and service.
	Using social media to introduce colleagues and contacts with shared scholarly interests	Establishing a social network of colleagues that can offer professional advice, emotional support, share resources, collaborate on teaching initiatives and/or research.

Indirect benefits from networking for service meeting more individual professional needs

Figure 6.1 The relationship between networking as a service and personal benefit.

The few examples above illustrate our understanding of how social networks are essentially dependent on linkages, relationships and information-sharing, and personal gains are a result thereof. Using tools such as social media platforms can allow valuable information to flow through the network and, in the process, enhance the reach and impact of research (Jordan, 2019). This form of networked participatory scholarship is further shown to enable the type of cross-disciplinary collaborations that reward scholars beyond their institutional roles (Stewart, 2015).

For digital scholars in leadership positions, such an understanding of social networking – with service and relationship-building as starting points – is also essential. It broadens their focus so that they can contextualise problems, draw from and contribute to broader bodies of knowledge, actively invest in relationships (more than relying on individual attributes) and continually learn from those beyond their apparent professional circle (Mccool et al., 2015). Unfortunately, many online social networks form organically to mirror pre-existing connections, rather than to seek engagement with new ones (Jordan, 2019). Those in leadership or other positions of power and influence can play an essential role in modelling an approach to networking that is open to a greater number of diverse voices.

6.3. Suggestions for next steps

- ✓ Start by considering the networks that share your values and professional objectives. Ask yourself what you can contribute to the network, in terms of your participation or sharing of resources.
- ✓ Once you have a better sense of the professional or social networks you want to engage with, find the relevant platforms to do so. This can include subscribing to a popular and well-established academic social networking site (ASNS), as well as to a non-academic, professional social networking (SNS) site.
- ✓ Create a well-rounded profile on each site. (For more details, refer to Table 6.1 'Practical suggestions for using social networking sites for digital scholarship'.)
- ✓ Try to find a balance between generating your own and sharing others' content. For sharing your own content, consider linking from the SNS to the ASNS where you upload your research outputs.
- ✓ If you are planning on hosting a synchronous (real-time) event such as a webinar, online workshop or conference, first attend a few of these sessions yourself. Note what kind of online activities, programme pacing and technical tools work, and what distracts from your networking experience. Refer to Table 6.2: *Practical suggestions relating to virtual conferences or online events* for more tips.

6.4   Conclusion

There is still much we do not understand about our networked practices in an increasingly digital and globalised society. The evolution of digital networking platforms is accompanied by ever-emerging needs for academics, such as on-demand and remote teaching, technical skills development, resource creation and technical support. There is a growing demand for academic content to be shared at an accelerated pace, and for teaching professionals and researchers to spend a larger portion of their working time online. While this chapter has predominantly focused on how digital networking can support the open and collaborative values of the digital scholar, we should also acknowledge that online networked practices have practical implications, and that they can in no way replace in-person social engagement.

Yet, the repercussions of the COVID-19 pandemic has shown (and is still showing) that we cannot afford to 'disconnect' from our scholarly communities and social networks. We are more interconnected and interdependent than ever, and we cannot address scientific, political or social issues without the collective action of rich and diverse global networks (Pepe et al., 2020). In previous chapters we discussed approaches for applying digital technologies in a variety of ways, related to our teaching, research and collaborative practices. Networking, as articulated in this chapter, calls for these activities to be connected to and to serve others within our institution, society or across global networks. Our networked practices may support our personal aspirations, but it will be most gratifying to see how, as we establish and strengthen relationships, our digital social networks become mechanisms for positive change.

References

Al Rawi, A. (2019). Viral News on Social Media. *Digital Journalism, 7*(1), 63–79.

Asmi, N. A., & Madhusudhan, M. (2015). Academic Social Networking Sites: What They Have to Offer for Researchers? *Journal of Knowledge & Communication Management, 5*(1), 1. https://doi.org/10.5958/2277-7946.2015.00001.7

Baker-Doyle, K. J. (2011). The networked teacher: How new teachers build social networks for professional suppor. Teachers College Press.

Boyd, D. M., & Ellison, N. B. (2007). Social network sites: Definition, history, and scholarship. *Journal of Computer-Mediated Communication, 13*(1), 210–230. https://doi.org/10.1111/j.1083-6101.2007.00393.x

Britton, B., Jackson, C., & Wade, J. (2019). The reward and risk of social media for academics. *Nature Reviews Chemistry, 3*(8), 459–461. https://doi.org/10.1038/s41570-019-0121-3

Brusilovsky, P., Oh, J. S., López, C., Parra, D., & Jeng, W. (2017). Linking information and people in a social system for academic conferences. *New Review of Hypermedia and Multimedia, 23*(2), 81–111. https://doi.org/10.1080/13614568.2016.1179796

Camedda, D., Mirman-Flores, A., & Ryan-Mangan, A. (2017). *Young researchers need help with academic networking.* University World News. https://www.universityworldnews.com/post.php?story=20170906091434215

Davis, B., & Sumara, D. (2009). Complexity as a theory of education. *TCI (Transnational Curriculum Inquiry), 5*(January 2009), 33–44. https://doi.org/ISSN: 1449-8855

Davis, N. L., Gough, M., & Taylor, L. L. (2019). Online teaching: advantages, obstacles and tools for getting it right. *Journal of Teaching in Travel and Tourism, 19*(3), 256–263. https://doi.org/10.1080/15313220.2019.1612313

Espinoza Vasquez, F. K., & Caicedo Bastidas, C. E. (2015). Academic Social Networking Sites: A Comparative Analysis of Their Services and Tools. *IConference*, 1–6.

Faucher, K. X. (2018). Social capital online: Alienation and accumulation (critical digital and social media studies). University of Westminster Press.

Fetterman, C. D. M. (2014). The SAGE Encyclopedia of Social Science Research Methods. 329–333.

Freeman, L. C. (2004). The Development of Social Network Analysis. BookSurge, LLC.

Gruzd, A., Haythornthwaite, C., Paulin, D., Gilbert, S., & del Valle, M. (2018). Uses and Gratifications factors for social media use in teaching: Instructors' perspectives. *New Media & Society, 20*(2), 475–494. https://doi.org/10.1177/1461444816662933

H. El-Shall, M. (2014). Net/working: higher education in the age of neoliberalism, crisis and social media. *Education + Training, 56*(7), 599–612. https://doi.org/10.1108/ET-07-2014-0080

Heidari, E., Salimi, G., & Mehrvarz, M. (2020). The influence of online social networks and online social capital on constructing a new graduate students' professional identity. *Interactive Learning Environments, 0*(0), 1–18. https://doi.org/10.1080/10494820.2020.1769682

Jordan, K. (2019). Separating and Merging Professional and Personal Selves Online: The Structure and Processes That Shape Academics' Ego-Networks on Academic Social Networking Sites and Twitter. *Journal of the Association for Information Science and Technology, 70*(8), 830–842. https://doi.org/10.1002/asi.24170

Jordan, K., & Weller, M. (2018). Communication, collaboration and identity: Factor analysis of academics' perceptions of online networking. *Research in Learning Technology, 26.* https://doi.org/10.25304/rlt.v26.2013

Kaltenbrunner, W. (2015). Scholarly Labour and Digital Collaboration in Literary Studies. *Social Epistemology, 29*(2), 207–233. https://doi.org/10.1080/02691728.2014.907834

Klöwer, M., Hopkins, D., Allen, M., & Higham, J. (2020). *An analysis of ways to decarbonize conference travel after COVID-19*. Nature. https://www.nature.com/articles/d41586-020-02057-2?sf236038067=1

Koopmans, M. (2017). Perspectives on Complexity, Its Definition and Applications in the Field. *Complicity, 14*(1), 16–35. -8&rfr_id=info:sid/ProQ%3Aeducation&rft_val_fmt=info:ofi/fmt:kev

Lessing, J. N., Anderson, L. R., Mark, N. M., Maggio, L. A., & Durning, S. J. (2020). Academics in Absentia: An Opportunity to Rethink Conferences in the Age of Coronavirus Cancellations. *Academic Medicine, 96*(12).

Levy, M., Hadar, I., Te'eni, D., Unkelos-Shpigel, N., Sherman, S., & Harel, N. (2016). Social networking in an academic conference context: insights from a case study. *Information Technology and People, 29*(1), 51–68. https://doi.org/10.1108/ITP-09-2014-0220

Lynch, T. (2011). Academic listening in the 21st century: Reviewing a decade of research. *Journal of English for Academic Purposes, 10*(2), 79–88. https://doi.org/10.1016/j.jeap.2011.03.001

Mainka, A., Hartmann, S., Stock, W. G., & Peters, I. (2015). Looking for friends and followers: A global investigation of governmental social media use. *Transforming Government: People, Process and Policy, 9*(2), 237–254. https://doi.org/10.1108/TG-09-2014-0041

Marin, A., & Wellman, B. (2016). Social Network Analysis: An Introduction. In J. Scott & P. J. Carriington (Eds.), *The SAGE Handbook of Social Network Analysis* (pp. 11–25). SAGE Publications.

Mccool, S. F., Freimund, W. A., Breen, C., Gorricho, J., Kohl, J., & Biggs, H. (2015). Benefiting From Complexity Thinking Benefiting From Complexity Thinking. *Protected Areas Governance and Management*, 291–326.

Meishar-Tal, H., & Pieterse, E. (2017). Why do academics use academic social networking sites? *International Review of Research in Open and Distance Learning, 18*(1), 1–22. https://doi.org/10.19173/irrodl.v18i1.2643

Ngware, M. (2020). Delivering education online: coronavirus underscores what's missing in Africa. The Conversation. https://theconversation. com/delivering-education-online-coronavirus-underscores-whats-missing-in-africa-134914.

Niner, H. J., Johri, S., Meyer, J., & Wassermann, S. N. (2020). The pandemic push: can COVID-19 reinvent conferences to models rooted in sustainability, equitability and inclusion? *Socio-Ecological Practice Research, 2*(3), 253–256. https://doi.org/10.1007/s42532-020-00059-y

Ovadia, S. (2014). ResearchGate and Academia.edu: Academic Social Networks. *Behavioral and Social Sciences Librarian, 33*(3), 165–169. https://doi.org/10.1080/01639269.2014.934093

Pepe, A., Cavalleri, M., Best, B., Olivotto, V., & Cantiello, M. (2020). Scientific collaboration in the era of COVID-19. *Authorea Preprints*, 1–8. https://doi.org/10.22541/au.158826951.14028294/v2

Pierpaolo, A. (2011). Complexity and Innovation. In P. Allen, S. Maguire, & B. McKelvey (Eds.), *The SAGE Handbook of Complexity and Management* (pp. 1–644). SAGE Publications. https://doi.org/10.4135/9781446201084

Quan-Haase, A., Martin, K., & McCay-Peet, L. (2015). Networks of digital humanities scholars: The informational and social uses and gratifications of Twitter. *Big Data and Society*, 2(1), 1–12. https://doi.org/10.1177/2053951715589417

Rowe, N. (2018). 'When You Get What You Want, But Not What You Need': The Motivations, Affordances and Shortcomings of Attending Academic/Scientific Conferences. *International Journal of Research in Education and Science*, 4(2), 714–729. https://doi.org/10.21890/ijres.438394

Scott, A., Woolcott, G., Keast, R., & Chamberlain, D. (2018). Sustainability of collaborative networks in higher education research projects: why complexity? Why now? *Public Management Review*, 20(7), 1068–1087. https://doi.org/10.1080/14719037.2017.1364410

Stewart, B. E. (2015). In abundance: networked participatory practices as scholarship. *The International Review of Research in Open and Distributed Learning*, 16(3). http://www.irrodl.org/index.php/irrodl/article/view/2158/3343

Thelwall, M., & Koucha, K. (2014). Academia.edu: Social Social Network or Academic Network? *Journal of the American Society for Information Science and Technology*, 65(4), 721–731. https://doi.org/10.1002/asi

Tsapali, M., & Paes, T. (2018). Social media for Academics and Early Career Researchers: An Interview with Dr Mark Carrigan. 5(November), 104–110.

Vandergriff, I. (2013). Emotive communication online: A contextual analysis of computer-mediated communication (CMC) cues. *Journal of Pragmatics*, 51, 1–12. https://doi.org/10.1016/j.pragma.2013.02.008

Veletsianos, G., & Kimmons, R. (2012). Networked Participatory Scholarship: Emergent techno-cultural pressures toward open and digital scholarship in online networks. *Computers and Education*, 58(2), 766–774. https://doi.org/10.1016/j.compedu.2011.10.001

Viskovic, A. (2006). Becoming a tertiary teacher: learning in communities of practice. *Higher Education Research and Development*, 25(4), 323–339. https://doi.org/10.1080/07294360600947285

Weller, M. (2011). *The Digital Scholar: How technology is transforming scholarly practice.* Bloomsbury academic. https://doi.org/10.5840/dspl2018111

Weller, M., Anderson, T., & Uk, M. (2013). Digital Resilience in Higher Education. *European Journal of Open, Distance and e-Learning*, 16(1). http://www.eurodl.org/?p=current&article=559

7
Professional Development Approaches for Digital Scholars: Taking ownership of your professional learning

Sonja Strydom

In this chapter we focus on

✓ An overview of the general practices associated with continuous professional development in the context of an evolving digital scholar.
✓ Three dimensions of continuous professional development.
✓ An overview of the different aspects that could potentially impact decisions to engage with continuous professional development.
✓ Different ways in which we can demonstrate our learning through critical reflection and the use of digital portfolios.

Keywords: Affordances; e-portfolios; knowledge; motivation; self-directed learning; self-regulated learning; professional development

7.1   Introduction

Engagement with digital technology, and then specifically digital scholarship, is an ongoing journey which cannot be limited to once-off or reductionist approaches that only focus on the use of digital tools in scholarly work. Due to the ever-evolving nature of digital technologies, we who acquaint ourselves with it need to understand that this is an ongoing commitment of exploration, critical selection, learning and evaluation. As can be expected, the nature of the digital world will then inevitably have an impact on the choices we make in terms of professional learning and the manner in which we choose to manage our learning opportunities. There are various factors, however, that we should consider and that could potentially inhibit us from continuously engaging with digitally related professional development. Factors could include limited resources, attitudes towards personal growth and learning, psychological factors or structural limitations, to name just a few.

Also, the manner in which we situate professional development of digital scholars could be at various levels, for example at an individual level, a group level or a departmental/faculty level. For the purpose of this chapter, the focus will remain mainly on ourselves at the individual level. In understanding how we, or then the 'agent', have influence on choices and approaches adopted in the professional learning process, the chapter offers a theoretical perspective that argues for an awareness of human agency and its related motivational factors. Building on agency and motivation, I argue that our actions, as displayed via self-directed and self-regulated learning, could guide us in the choices we make in relation to professional learning as digital scholars. Finally, I guide your attention to the practices linked with different types of e-portfolios and the notion of reflection to lead us in future initiatives and applying our newly acquired knowledge.

7.2   Continuous professional development

One of the key learnings in especially the field of educational technology is that learning never stops. Surrounded by a world of ever-evolving digital devices, new approaches to learning, increasingly sophisticated hardware and software and the fourth industrial revolution, there will always be opportunity to increase our knowledge and understanding of the digital world. Such a dynamic context, therefore, asks of us to be cognisant of the embeddedness of continuous professional development as part and parcel of our 'armour' as digital scholars.

The literature often uses different terms interchangeably to communicate our quest for further learning and development. Such terminology could include 'academic development', 'educational development', 'staff development', 'staff training', 'professional development' and so forth (Clegg, 2009). The aim of this chapter is not to delineate these concepts, nor to attempt to uncover the semantic differences of each. Rather, I mention these terms to sensitise you towards the realisation that digital scholars should continuously engage in further learning initiatives – irrespective of the terminology used for the endeavour of broadening and applying our knowledge of digital technologies. For the purpose of this chapter, I will be referring to 'continuous professional development' (CPD) to underline the embedded nature of further growth and knowledge in the field of educational technology.

Identifying potential areas of further knowledge development can be daunting. This is even more so the case in a digital world since tools and practices change regularly. I suggest that we critically consider our professional development trajectory. In the next section, I will be focusing on three potential levels of professional development (see Table 7.1).

One way of starting our professional development journey is to ensure that we have a solid overview of the tools and approaches currently available. Such a focus could, for instance, further develop our technical knowledge related to the different digital tools. It will be at this level that we have to decide for ourselves which tools are most appropriate for our particular contextual needs. If we are engaged in education, the next level outcome could, for instance, be to further enhance our pedagogical knowledge and its application with digital technologies. At this level we can, for example, critically consider the teaching philosophies we hold and how we believe learning takes place. Through such self-reflective practices, we will then potentially be better positioned to apply our digital knowledge to our pedagogical knowledge. The final level could consist of looking forward to and further planning of our professional development, since we argued that we would likely need to commit to a continuous view of learning in a digital world.

Three dimensions of continuous professional development	
Outcome: Gaining insight and understanding into the myriad tools and approaches related to digital technology	*Focus:* Digital knowledge
Outcome: Considering pedagogical approaches associated with digital technologies	*Focus:* Pedagogical knowledge
Outcome: Identifying and assessing potential avenues for further learning opportunities	*Focus:* Vehicle for further knowledge development

Table 7.1: Three dimensions of continuous professional development as a digital scholar.

7.2.1 Digital knowledge: Digital tools and their affordances

The evolution of the world wide web also contributes to the growth of different online tools and other related products to serve users. Web 1.0 focused on the delivery of content where read-only interaction was required. Web 2.0, on the other hand, built on its predecessor and supports the development of social networks, collaboration, the creation and substitution of content and a general requirement that users become actively involved in online activities. It is with the evolution of Web 3.0 that we will be able to make meaning of large data sets where it will provide opportunity for machines to communicate the data into comprehensible formats to users (Miranda, Isaias, Costa, & Pifano, 2017). As we can expect, these changes will have an

139

Figure 7.1: Typology of free web-based digital technologies (Bower & Torrington, 2020, p.2).

impact over time on the manner in which we approach our digital scholarship. The affordances associated with the web, as it evolves over time, will influence the way we approach teaching and learning, the manner in which we expect students to engage with digital learning approaches and devices, and also the methods we consider in our own personal practices.

The effect and use of Web 2.0 are still prevalent in our daily practices and are still relevant in, for instance, the educational sphere. Many of us are still in our infancy shoes when engaging with digital technologies. Therefore, it is important that we have an overview of the available online tools and how they could be aligned with learning and teaching practices. Bower and Torrington (2020) developed a useful typology of accessible online tools (see Figure 7.1) that could be used in educational practices. I share this typology with you to guide you towards your own identification of the aspects that you need further training and development in. The typology demonstrates the necessity to gain an overview of what is available and then to make informed decisions about how and where you would like to gain further knowledge and experience in these approaches and tools. The criteria that the authors used were as follows:

- ✓ It should be free and not only for a trial version.
- ✓ The tools should be accessible via the use of a web-browser.
- ✓ The tools should provide users with the opportunity to collaborate and share content.
- ✓ It should be appropriate for educational purposes (Bower & Torrington, 2020, p. 3).

The different collections and their affordances are outlined in the next table (Table 7.2). This typology could assist us in determining the area of further development as well as its associated applications in our teaching and learning, or professional practices.

Free web-based learning technologies	Affordances
Text based tools	Synchronous text discussion
	Discussion forums
	Note-taking and document creation
Image based tools	Image sharing
	Image creation and editing
	Drawing and painting
	Online whiteboarding
	Diagramming
	Mind mapping
	Mapping
	Word clouds
Audio tools	Audio sharing
	Audio creation and editing
Video tools	Video sharing
	Video creation and editing
	Video streaming
Multimodal production tools	Digital pinboards
	Presentations
	Lesson authoring
Digital storytelling tools	Online book creation
	Comic strip creation
	Animated videos

Website creation tools	Individual website creation
	Wikis
	Blogs
Knowledge organisation and sharing tools	File sharing
	Social bookmarking
	Aggregators
	Republishing
	Timeline creators
Data analysis tools	Conducting surveys
	Online spreadsheets
	Infographics
3D Modelling tools	3D repositories
	3D model creation
Coding tools	
Assessment tools	
Social networking systems	
Learning Management Systems	
Web-conferencing tools	

Table 7.2: Free web-based learning technologies: Typology collections (Bower & Torrington, 2020, p.3-12).

7.2.2 *Pedagogical knowledge: Pedagogical approaches associated with digital technologies*

Digital knowledge is only one aspect that we need to continuously develop. If we are engaged in education, the next step is to ensure that we are able to align our digital knowledge with the manner in which we approach teaching and learning. This topic, however, does not enjoy much prominence in the literature and is often segmented in terms of a focus on a specific tool and its associated learning activity. When we think about CPD and aligning our knowledge of digital technologies and pedagogical knowledge, a more structured approach should be considered. In the next section I will make some suggestions of the type of questions we can ask ourselves to assist ourselves in thinking about our own professional development needs.

Firstly, I suggest that we consider the *level* of technology integration that we are hoping to achieve in our teaching. Are we thinking about a broad approach which implies that we need to rethink or redesign an entire module or unit of work, or will we start small with one or two interventions?

142

Level

✓ *Macro level:* You want to redesign your whole module or unit of work with the integration of digital technologies where appropriate. This means that you need to consider critically the different learning and assessment activities and how it aligns with your course learning outcomes.

✓ *Micro level:* You would like to try out one approach or a small set of tools to get started. For example, you could decide to explore the notion of increased student engagement via in-class digital responses. This would mean that you need to identify a particular online tool (e.g., Kahoot) and identify sections of the work where such an approach would be educationally appropriate.

To be able to respond to the level of technology integration, we need to have a general overview of the *tools and learning approaches* available to be considered. We have discussed this in the previous section related to digital tools and their affordances. There is, however, also another important aspect that we need to align with our technological knowledge: our understanding of how student learning takes place. This implies that we need to ensure that we have a good grasp of the basic learning theories associated with our cohort and how these align with digital technology use. It is only when we understand the interplay between learning and actions required by students that we will be able to seamlessly integrate tools and approaches in the chosen learning and assessment activities.

Digital tools and learning approaches

✓ Ensure that you have a general overview of the types of digital technologies available for educational purposes (see the previous section in the chapter).

✓ Select tools that you deem appropriate and confirm that you are aware of the affordances of each of these tools.

✓ Critically consider how these digital tools could be integrated into learning or assessment activities while you take cognisance of existing learning theories that you align your teaching practices with.

Upskill yourself in a working knowledge of the chosen digital tools. It is always better to understand how each of the digital tools that you consider works before encouraging your students to make use of it.

Digital skills

✓ Ensure that you have a working knowledge of each of the digital tools that you expect your students to be using in their course.
✓ Practise and test the tool before sharing it with your students.

A large part of the success of the learning intervention is also reliant on the level of support that we provide for *students*. This includes technical as well as educational support. In terms of technical support, it is advisable that we ensure that we have a step-by-step guide available for students to consult when they are unsure how to use a particular tool. It is also good practice to create a short demonstration video as an alternative level of support to those students who prefer a visual aid. In terms of course-related queries, clearly indicate to your students who to ask for help, when assistance will be available, and when they could expect feedback on their queries.

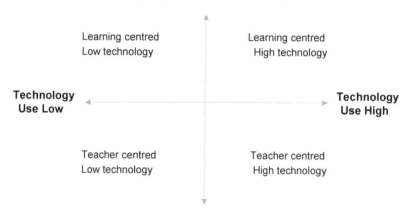

Figure 7.2: Teaching approaches and digital technology use.
Source: Adapted from https://teach.com/what/teachers-know/teaching-methods/

Student support

✓ Develop a step-by-step technical support guide for students combined with a short instructional video.

✓ Ensure that your students are aware of where to access support for course-related queries.

When you have considered the above, you will be able to plot your teaching approaches with digital technology on the plane presented in Figure 7.2. With your understanding of how learning takes place and what you expect of your students, you will be able to indicate your general activities on the y axis that suggests the extent of the different learning approaches. On the x axis, you can refer back to the level of technology integration that you are considering for your particular course or unit. This will assist you in indicating where you currently are in terms of your preferred technology use.

In relation to our professional development as digital scholars, it will be interesting to observe how we move through the different quadrants of the plane. It is not suggested that any of these planes is more preferred than another, but rather that it could serve as a reflective tool to assist you in your potential future professional learning activities.

7.2.3 Vehicle for further knowledge development: Exploring different avenues for learning

There are many possible avenues to consider when wanting to further your knowledge and skills. Web-based learning opportunities are growing at a steady rate and provide us with endless choices.

Massive open online courses (MOOCs) and small private online courses (SPOCs) could be a consideration if you are thinking about a more structured learning opportunity where you have the option to obtain formal recognition for your learning. Academics, experts and even non-experts have a wide range of courses to choose from. Some of the well-known service providers of these courses include Coursera, LinkedIn Learning and Udemy. As mentioned earlier in the chapter, you will also need to take ownership of obtaining as much information as possible about the courses and topics available before you make a choice. For instance, would you like to pay for the course, or are you looking for free learning opportunities? What about qualifications or types of certificates? Do you need a certificate of participation or completion of a course? Be aware that in many cases you would need to pay for a certificate of recognition.

Some examples of different levels of recognition that you can expect:

No certificate
No certificate, only open badges
Only open badges and a paid verified certificate
Open badges and a fee certificate that serves as a statement of accomplishment
A formal record of achievement and/or a digital badge
A free certificate that states your accomplishment
A free certificate or a verified certificate
A paid statement of participation

Table 7.3: Types of recognition in online courses
(Source: https://www.mooc-list.com/types-of-certificates)

Colorado State University (2014) provides a useful beginner's guide to free online courses which might be of benefit to you if you are not familiar with all the possibilities available.[62]

If you are not looking for a structured learning opportunity, you might consider *webinars,* where institutions or individuals offer short learning or discussion opportunities based on a particular topic. These learning opportunities afford us the opportunity not to commit to a long-term learning intervention and also possibly to engage with like-minded individuals also participating in the webinar. These sessions are often also a good platform to build professional networks.

Additionally, you could also sign up for particular *subscriptions* where you will receive regular updates and news in your inbox. These opportunities are mostly based on enrichment or broadening our knowledge in a particular field, but could also serve as a platform to advertise upcoming courses, webinars or conferences that might be of interest.

From an institutional perspective, you always have the opportunity to sign up for *formalised institutional initiatives* which provide you with the opportunity to build knowledge on topics that are prioritised by your institution. In this case, topics will usually be aligned with institutional goals or directives where we could directly feed newly acquired knowledge and skills back into our department or community of professionals. In some cases, such initiatives could be formal accredited short courses or one-day sessions where you receive relevant information in digestible chunks.

7.3 Aspects associated with digital technology use

There are a wide range of factors impacting whether we will choose to engage with continuous professional development as digital scholars. Such factors could be complex, multifaceted and context-specific.

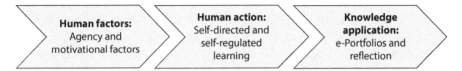

Figure 7.3: Understanding professional learning in preparation for sustainable digital scholarship and development

In this next section I will draw your attention to some of these aspects and how they relate to the choices we make in terms of continuous professional development. Firstly, I will provide you with an overview of the role and nature of agency and our perceived levels of self-efficacy and how this could impact our actions towards professional development. I will also provide you with a short overview of the role of motivational factors. Secondly, I will briefly focus your attention on the importance of self-directed and self-regulated learning. The section will provide you with an overview of these concepts and how it affects our choices in terms of professional development. Lastly, the section will conclude with highlighting some practices on how you could apply your newly acquired knowledge by means of reflective practices and the use of an e-portfolio system.

7.3.1 *Human factors related to continuous professional development choices*

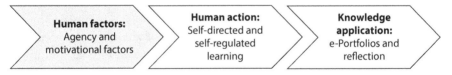

Figure 7.3.1: Understanding professional learning in preparation for sustainable digital scholarship and development: Human factors.

7.3.1.1 *Role of agency*
Agency relates to the fact that humans act with purpose, are proactive and are in control of their chosen actions and motivation (Bandura & Locke,

2003). Most of us are aware of agency at an individual level. However, according to the social-cognitive theory, there are three types of agency, namely personal, proxy and collective. The literature tends to focus on individual agency and how cognitive, motivational and social factors impact such actions. Sometimes, individuals do not have influence over their institutional circumstances or broader social context. In such a case we could adopt proxy agency where we rely on other individuals that do have the perceived influence or expertise to represent us. Collective agency, on the other hand, places influence in the hands of a particular group (Bandura, 2000). The importance of understanding the different levels of agency lies in our approach to professional development and our own learning. We could see our journey as digital scholars as an individual pursuit where we act in isolation and our own needs. Contrary to this, it might be that you are working in an environment where you need to convince others of the importance of digital scholarship and learning. It is in such circumstances that proxy agency could be of relevance. And, lastly, collective agency could be of value in any circumstances where you function as part of a group. It could be departmental team, working with teaching colleagues, or even professionals working together on one particular project. The influence as a group can then become of value in considering and approaching different learning opportunities as digital scholars.

7.3.1.2 *Motivational explanations*

Different motivational factors could impact our actions towards continuous professional development as digital scholars. Such factors could include those things that we need, what we expect as well as the way in which we think about further learning practices. In the following section I provide a short overview of some of these factors and how they could potentially relate to the choices we make in terms of our own learning.

Our responses towards our agentic choices are often rooted in our *perceived level of self-efficacy*. A lot of our human behaviour is influenced by our thoughts about future success or the possibility of attaining our identified goals. The ways in which we think about potential success or goal attainment have an impact on our perceived self-efficacy. Those of us that display high levels of self-efficacy will visualise success and the ability to reach set goals. Low self-efficacy levels, on the other hand, persuade us to anticipate limited levels of success and potential failure (Bandura, 1993). The manner in which these psychological thought processes impact our beliefs about continuous professional learning – specifically in the field of digital technologies – will possibly also contribute to the way we approach our own learning goals.

148

Those of us that display lower levels of self-efficacy can potentially think that it is unlikely that we will be able to master certain tools, device usage or even methods associated with digital technologies, and will be hesitant to approach the continuous learning journey with a 'can do' attitude. Our self-efficacy beliefs are based on a complex combination of motivational, cognitive, affective and personal decision procedures that impact our chosen actions (Bandura & Locke, 2003). Say, for instance, you are considering enrolling for an online course – your perceived level of self-efficacy could influence whether you will decide to spend the time and energy as part of your professional development. If you have high levels of self-efficacy, you will believe that you can be successful and that you are able to reach the goals you've set out for yourself in terms of the course or your general professional development.

The expectancy-value theory also provides us with insights into our motivation to engage with CPD. According to this theoretical perspective, your expectations as well as the value you ascribe to achieving your goal will impact your actions. In other words, this theory highlights your perceptions about how well you can complete a particular task or activity and the rationale for wanting to complete the activity – the value you place on the activity (Panchal, Adesope, & Malak, 2012; Wigfield & Eccles, 2000). Our expectancies, needs and values all contribute to the complex processes of deciding to engage with continuous professional development or not. This could be explained as follows:

Motivation = Perceived probability of success in a task x subject task value (Panchal et al., 2012).

If we draw on our example of enrolment in the online course, your perceived probability of completing the online course will be one of the factors determining your choice to participate. If you do think that the course is too difficult or that there are other possible reasons why you will not be able to complete it, your perceived level of success will be low. Similarly, if success in the completion of the course is of particular value to you based on, for instance, promotion or being able to apply your newly acquired knowledge in a teaching and learning context, your motivational levels to enrol for such a course will be higher than if you thought the course was of no outstanding value to you.

Another possible explanation could be the manner in which our actions and beliefs of success could be closely aligned with our particular needs. According to the achievement motivation theory, we are motivated to act based on our *need for achievement, need for power and need for affiliation.* This is called the achievement motivation theory (Moore, Grabsch, & Rotter, 2010). McClelland (1961) posits that a need for achievement showcases our need to be successful in some form of contest where we display a level of excellence. It implies that when we consider, for instance, to enrol in an online course we will be able to "accomplish something difficult, attain a high standard of success, master complex tasks, and surpass others" (Daft, 2008, as cited in Moore et al., 2010, p. 25). The need for power is often displayed as a way by which we would like to display a level of authority by wanting to lead and demonstrate influence (Moore et al., 2010). Lastly, our need for affiliation (McClelland, 1961) implies that we value close relationships or interaction with other people. In relation to our example of participation in an online course, it could, for instance, imply that we will consider enrolling for the course if we will succeed in showcasing our newly acquired expertise (i.e., need for power) and that we will be able to participate in the course as members of a group of scholars or peers (i.e., need for affiliation). In other words, if we choose to sign up for an online course, we will probably only enrol if we are sure that we will be successful and that the course itself contributes to what we perceive as important in our quest towards continuous professional development.

These are only three possible reasons or motivational factors that could potentially influence the choices you make in relation to continuous professional development. Human motivation and action are clearly complex and multifaceted and can be influenced by a number of factors. This section aimed only to sensitise you towards some of the possible reasons.

7.3.2 *Human action and digital technology*
Apart from understanding the possible motivational factors that could influence our deliberations regarding CPD, we also need to consider the responsibility that will inevitably rest on our shoulders when we start to engage with our different initiatives. Self-directed and self-regulated learning will be of relevance during the different professional learning initiatives that we embark on, but can also be significant when we view our professional development at a meta level.

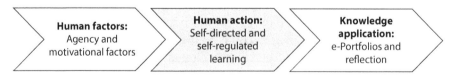

Figure 7.3.2: Understanding professional learning in preparation for sustainable digital scholarship and development: Human action.

7.3.2.1 Self-directed and self-regulated learning

The way in which adults learn has been a research topic for many years. There is no one model, framework or explanation to succinctly outline the processes of how and when learning takes place (Ellinger, 2004). In order for us to become lifelong learners that take responsibility for our own learning by continuously engaging with professional development, we can consider the importance of the notion and act of self-directed learning (SDL) and self-regulated learning (SRL).

SDL and SRL are often used synonymously, but do refer to two separate ways of learning (Jossberger, Brand-Gruwel, Boshuizen, & van de Wiel, 2010). Both these constructs relate the importance of being actively involved in the learning process by clarifying desired outcomes, the ability of learners to choose learning approaches that will be applicable to the context and the awareness of assessment of learning goals (Gandomkar & Sandars, 2018).

SDL could be explained as "self-learning in which learners have the primary responsibility for planning, carrying out, and evaluating their learning experiences" (Ellinger, 2004, p. 159). It means that the learner has the skill to design a learning environment that is appropriate for his or her learning needs (Saks & Leijen, 2014). This approach to learning is mostly situated at a macro level where the learner takes responsibility for developing a specific learning trajectory appropriate for the learning needs to be accomplished (Jossberger et al., 2010). The types of skills that someone will display when engaged with SDL are the ability to know what to learn next, being able to articulate the specific learning outcome, identifying the needed resources to support the learning process and to monitor the activities (Saks & Leijen, 2014). This type of learning can take place in formal or informal settings and learners can draw on the expertise of others and external resources to accomplish their goals (Ellinger, 2004).

In the context of developing as a digital scholar, SDL will imply that you adopt a specific learning approach that suits you in terms of the educational goal you would like to achieve (Gandomkar & Sandars, 2018). For instance, it might be that you've decided that you need to improve your knowledge and skills related to technology-augmented pedagogies. It means that you would look at your learning trajectory for an academic year and identify the different aspects needed for you to achieve such a goal. By seeing the 'bigger picture' at a macro level, you might decide that the first step would be to gain an overview of some of the popular pedagogies related to digital technology. Secondly, you decide that it is necessary for you to upskill yourself in terms of two new digital approaches in terms of technical training. And, lastly, you conclude that you will apply your newly acquired knowledge gained through your two previous learning goals by applying it to a post-graduate class that you are teaching in the second semester. You choose to design your learning environment by signing up for a massive open online course (MOOC) to learn about the different pedagogical approaches associated with digital pedagogies and ask for the help of your digital technologies team in identifying possible digital tools that could assist you in your quest. Lastly, you could make use of the advice of an academic developer to help you design your learning interventions for your postgraduate teaching group. Through this process, you were able to design a specific learning trajectory appropriate for your unique learning needs.

Self-regulated learning (SRL), on the other hand, is an approach that you adopt when focusing on a clearly defined goal or task (Gandomkar & Sandars, 2018). It consists of forethought, performance and self-reflection (Beaumont, Moscrop, & Canning, 2016), and is mostly involved in the manner in which you will complete or execute a particular task (Saks & Leijen, 2014). SRL is a process where there is a clear beginning and end and where you make use of an active cycle of re-assessment and adaptation (Gandomkar & Sandars, 2018). These processes will include cognitive, motivational and metacognitive activities (Gandomkar & Sandars, 2018, p. 862).

When you have a particular task to complete, it will imply that you will first decide if the task is easy or difficult based on the nature of the task as well as your own cognitive appraisal. Secondly you will decide on the particular standards that will guide you towards the appropriate actions you would need to take to complete the task successfully. The next step would be to consider specific learning activities that will lead to the desired outcomes. You will then assess those outcomes with your own internal standards. Lastly, it might mean that your performance will also be assessed by external feedback or evaluation (Sun, Xie, & Anderman, 2018).

If we use the example of the suggested learning trajectory in the previous section, it could mean that you've decided to learn how to create an online video as part of a digital story (the second learning goal discussed in self-directed learning). Firstly, you will decide whether it is easy or difficult to learn how to use particular video editing software. You determine that you would like to be able to create a video with voice narration and background music, which implies that there are specific technical aspects you would need to familiarise yourself with. When considering the specific learning activities associated with the task, it could be that you need to know where to find music for the background and the factors needed to be considered when making use of narration in a video. After your efforts in combining music and voice, you will look at the product and decide, based on your own standards, if you were successful in the task or not.

7.3.3 Knowledge application: Translating learning into practice

Another aspect to consider is how we start to integrate and apply our newly acquired knowledge in our different contexts. A suggestion is to carefully consider the value of reflection and sharing your beliefs and skills in the format of a digital or e-portfolio.

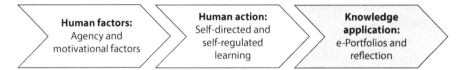

Figure 7.3.3: Understanding professional learning in preparation for sustainable digital scholarship and development: Knowledge Application.

7.3.3.1 e-Portfolios and reflection

There are different ways in which we can share our professional development, teaching and learning practices or even our teaching philosophies in a discursive online space. The use of an electronic portfolio (e-portfolios) could be considered for these practices. As Pitts and Ruggirello (2012, p. 50) explain: "Viewed conceptually, e-portfolios are multimedia spaces that afford users the capacity to analyse and illustrate growth within the discourse and standards of a community. Within this discursive space the network of evidence used to illustrate growth and change is interlinked via the capacity to simultaneously illustrate and conceptualise practice over time." The use of portfolios is a useful tool and approach that could assist in the practice of continuous professional development, since it places emphasis on the significance of social learning and reflection (Tigelaar et al., 2009). e-Portfolios could be used to demonstrate the attainment of specific attributes and skills through the processes of reflection and continuous professional development (Carl & Strydom, 2017). It is argued that "reflection and lifelong learning emphasise both the processes and skills required to continually seek, acquire, renew, and upgrade knowledge skills, competencies and attitudes" (Gordon & Campbell, 2013, p. 288).

There are different types of e-portfolios with distinct goals in mind. These usually include a demonstration of learning, to showcase a particular product of learning or to reflect on learning experiences. Different types of e-portfolios are in use with terminology often used interchangeably to explain these portfolios. For the purpose of this chapter, we will consider teaching portfolios, reflective portfolios and professional development portfolios.

Teaching portfolios originated from teacher training, where emphasis is placed on providing evidence of specific teaching experiences. The purpose of these portfolios is usually to demonstrate attributes and skills and to provide evidence for promotion or accreditation purposes. This type of portfolio typically starts with a declaration of the user's teaching philosophy and the way in which you consider approaches to teaching and learning as well as professional development. The teaching portfolio could also be used to demonstrate alternative training routes that were followed to achieve teaching status, references to membership of professional bodies or any other postgraduate qualifications that were obtained in the light of the professional context. Different types of teaching portfolios exist. For instance, apart from the individual portfolio, course portfolios could focus on the development of one particular course. At a broader level, a departmental portfolio could be aligned with administrative, learning and/or assessment goals (Lai, Lim, & Wang, 2016).

Reflective portfolios could also form part of a teaching portfolio. For the purpose of this section, however, I will address this as a separate type of portfolio and approach. As the name suggests, these types of portfolios underline and embrace the importance of reflective writing practices by sharing personal reflections of different learning journeys or actions. Various multimedia artefacts could be used to share the different reflections. The reflective portfolio usually consists of a record of the different learning activities and the associated rationale for each. Through reflective writing techniques, the user shares responses to the learning activities and their future implications. These portfolios form the basis of a compilation of reflective activities demonstrating a specific learning journey over time.

As mentioned in the above, the practice of reflection plays a valuable part in the learning journeys of individuals. It enables us to "express ideals for better, deeper, more liberating ways of learning" (Van Woerkom, 2008, p. 3). However, the notion of reflection is often differently described in the literature (Van Woerkom, 2004), which complicates an attempt to provide you with a succinct definition or description. For instance, in the earlier explanations, Dewey (1938) argued that an emotive component was aligned with being reflective, Schön (1975) placed emphasis on the value to the institution when employees engage with reflective actions, while Boud, Keogh and Walker (1985) are of the opinion that individual learning comes to the fore through reflective practices (Carl & Strydom, 2017, p. 2).

Terms which are regularly used interchangeably are reflection, critical reflection and critical thinking. Often, the differences between these terms are unclear. To complicate matters, there are many reflective models and practices in the literature, and I will not attempt to provide you with an overview, nor to suggest one particular approach to consider. Rather, for the purpose of this section, I will briefly sensitise you towards the practice of reflection and will make suggestions how this practice could feed into your professional learning activities as a digital scholar. Despite the possible confusion and differing opinions, it becomes clear that learning is the essence of reflective practices. Attention is paid to a specific incident where opportunities are created for individuals to expand their knowledge and experience (Carl & Strydom, 2017).

Professional development portfolios are appropriate to demonstrate the development of attributes and skills associated with professional practice and personal development planning (PDP) (Ahmed & Ward, 2016). Self-directed learning principles are key to the effective and continuous use of a professional development portfolio. Usually, the professional development practices associated with the use of such a portfolio consist of an identification of the unique professional learning needs of the user, the development of a personal development plan (PDP), identifying avenues to implement the PDP and, lastly, an assessment of learning and skills acquired via reflective practices (Foucault, Vachon, Thomas, Rochette, & Giguère, 2018). The main purpose of the use of such a portfolio and learning approach is to assist the user in their individual and collective professional activities (Foucault et al., 2018). It implies that the users take responsibility for their own professional development trajectory.

Type of portfolio	Focus	Typical sections
Digital teaching portfolio (DTP)	Teaching philosophy Share your general approach to T&L and professional development Evidence of alternative approaches to achieving accreditation, membership of professional bodies or postgraduate qualifications	Teaching philosophy statement Evidence of teaching performance and impact Planning and preparation Student learning assessment Evidence of professional development and future plans
Reflective portfolio	Using various multimedia artefacts to share personal reflections on a learning journey	Listing of learning purposes Responses to learning activities Compilation of reflective activities
Electronic professional development portfolio (e-PDP)	Professional development planning (PDP) focusing on learning and development opportunities Demonstrating continuous engagement with learning activities Reflective practices associated with learning opportunities	Demonstration of products associated with learning Emphasis on the process of learning via retrospective reflective practices Consideration of prospective actions required for professional development

Table 7.4: Different types of portfolios to demonstrate learning as a digital scholar
Source: Consortium (2004); Foucault et al. (2018); Hughes & Moore (2007); Lai et al. (2016); Strivens (2007).

An important part of CPD is to have the ability to view your professional learning trajectory objectively and to demonstrate further areas for development through the processes of critical reflection. As mentioned earlier, by engaging in digital scholarship it will be possibly expected of you to adopt a flexible approach to continuous learning, based on the evolving nature of the field, its associated practices and the digital tools available.

7.4   Suggested way forward

- ✓ Identify the dimension of professional development (digital knowledge, pedagogical knowledge or further knowledge development) where you would like to start broadening your professional learning journey.
- ✓ Explore a 'new' digital tool that you have not used previously.
- ✓ Consider the use of an e-portfolio as a process or product orientated resource to showcase and reflect on your learning.

7.5   Conclusion

Embracing the digital world and growing as a digital scholar requires of us to embrace the notion of continuous professional development. It implies that we become aware of the different dimensions associated with CPD and the manner in which we choose to position an individualised learning trajectory appropriate for our own individual, scholarly or institutional needs. It is only by being aware of the aspects associated with digital use that we will start to understand our approaches to continuous learning. By identifying and being cognisant of our attitudes towards agency and motivation, the way in which we approach learning and the value placed on critical reflection and knowledge application, could pave the way for a scholarly journey of new insights, skills and attributes closely aligned with the requirements of a world filled with digital technologies and related approaches.

References

Ahmed, E., & Ward, R. (2016). Analysis of factors influencing acceptance of personal, academic and professional development e-portfolios. *Computers in Human Behavior, 63,* 152–161. https://doi.org/10.1016/j.chb.2016.05.043

Bandura, A. (1993). Perceived Self-Efficacy in Cognitive Development and Functioning. *Educational Psychologist*. https://doi.org/10.1207/s15326985ep2802_3

Bandura, A. (2000). Exercise of Human Agency Through Collective Efficacy. *Current Directions in Psychological Science*, *9*(3), 75–78. https://doi.org/10.1111/1467-8721.00064

Bandura, A., & Locke, E. a. (2003). Negative self-efficacy and goal effects revisited. *The Journal of Applied Psychology*, *88*(1), 87–99. https://doi.org/10.1037/0021-9010.88.1.87

Beaumont, C., Moscrop, C., & Canning, S. (2016). Easing the transition from school to HE: scaffolding the development of self-regulated learning through a dialogic approach to feedback. *Journal of Further and Higher Education*, *40*(3), 331–350. https://doi.org/10.10 80/0309877X.2014.953460

Bower, M., & Torrington, J. (2020). Typology of Free Web-based Learning Technologies, (April), 15. Retrieved from https://library.educause.edu/resources/2020/4/typology-of-free-web-based-learning-technologies

Carl, A., & Strydom, S. (2017). e-Portfolio as Reflection Tool during Teaching Practice: The Interplay between Contextual and Dispositional Variables. *South African Journal of Education*, *37*(1), 1–10. https://doi.org/10.15700/saje.v37n1a1250

Clegg, S. (2009). Forms of knowing and academic development practice. *Studies in Higher Education*, *34*(4), 403–416. https://doi.org/10.1080/03075070902771937

Consortium, S. (2004). Reparing your teaching portfolio, (2003), 1–7.

Ellinger, A. D. (2004). The Concept of Self-Directed Learning and Its Implications for Human Resource Development. *Advances in Developing Human Resources*, *6*(2), 158–177. https://doi.org/10.1177/1523422304263327

Foucault, M. L., Vachon, B., Thomas, A., Rochette, A., & Giguère, C. É. (2018). Utilisation of an electronic portfolio to engage rehabilitation professionals in continuing professional development: results of a provincial survey. *Disability and Rehabilitation*, *40*(13), 1591–1599. https://doi.org/10.1080/09638288.2017.1300335

Gandomkar, R., & Sandars, J. (2018). Clearing the confusion about self-directed learning and self-regulated learning. *Medical Teacher*, *40*(8), 862–863. https://doi.org/10.1080/01 42159X.2018.1425382

Gordon, J. A., & Campbell, C. M. (2013). The role of ePortfolios in supporting continuing professional development in practice. *Medical Teacher*, *35*(4), 287–294. https://doi.org/10 .3109/0142159X.2013.773395

Hughes, J., & Moore, I. (2007). Reflective portfolios for professional development. In C. O'Farrell (Ed.), *Teaching portfolio practice in Ireland: A handbook* (pp. 11–23). Dublin: Centre for Academic Practice and Student Learning.

Jossberger, H., Brand-Gruwel, S., Boshuizen, H., & van de Wiel, M. (2010). The challenge of self-directed and self-regulated learning in vocational education: A theoretical analysis and synthesis of requirements. *Journal of Vocational Education and Training*, *62*(4), 415–440. https://doi.org/10.1080/13636820.2010.523479

Lai, M., Lim, C. P., & Wang, L. (2016). Potential of digital teaching portfolios for establishing a professional learning community in higher education. *Australasian Journal of Educational Technology*, *32*(2), 1–14. https://doi.org/10.14742/ajet.2572

Miranda, P., Isaias, P., Costa, J. C., & Pifano, S. (2017). Validation of an e-learning 3.0 critical success factors framework: A qualitative research. *Journal of Information Technology Education: Research*, *16*, 339–363. Retrieved from http://www.informingscience.org/Publications/3865

Moore, L. L., Grabsch, D. K., & Rotter, C. (2010). Using Achievement Motivation Theory to Explain Student Participation in a Residential Leadership Learning Community. *Journal of Leadership Education*, *9*(2), 22–34. https://doi.org/10.12806/v9/i2/rf2

Panchal, J. H., Adesope, O., & Malak, R. (2012). Designing undergraduate design experiences-A framework based on the expectancy-value theory. *International Journal of Engineering Education*, *28*(4), 871–879.

Pitts, W., & Ruggirello, R. (2012). Using the e-Portfolio to Document and Evaluate Growth in Reflective Practice: The Development and Application of a Conceptual Framework. *International Journal of E-Portfolio*, *2*(1), 49–74.

Saks, K., & Leijen, Ä. (2014). Distinguishing Self-directed and Self-regulated Learning and Measuring them in the E-learning Context. *Procedia – Social and Behavioral Sciences*, *112*(Iceepsy 2013), 190–198. https://doi.org/10.1016/j.sbspro.2014.01.1155

Strivens, J. (2007). A survey of e-pdp and e-portfolio practice in UK Higher Education. Retrieved October 10, 2020, from https://www.advance-he.ac.uk/knowledge-hub/survey-e-pdp-and-e-portfolio-practice-uk-higher-education

Sun, Z., Xie, K., & Anderman, L. H. (2018). The role of self-regulated learning in students' success in flipped undergraduate math courses. *Internet and Higher Education*, *36*(June 2017), 41–53. https://doi.org/10.1016/j.iheduc.2017.09.003

Tigelaar, D. E. H., Dolmans, D. H. J. M., Grave, W. S. De, Ineke, H. A. P., Van, C. P. M., Tigelaar, D. E. H., … Grave, W. S. De. (2009). Portfolio as a tool to stimulate teachers ' reflections Portfolio as a tool to stimulate teachers ' reflections. https://doi.org/10.1080/01421590600607013

van Woerkom, M. (2004). The Concept of Critical Reflection and Its Implications for Human Resource Development. *Advances in Developing Human Resources*, *6*(2), 178–192. https://doi.org/10.1177/1523422304263328

van Woerkom, M. (2008). Critical reflection and related higher-level conceptualizations of learning: Realistic or idealistic? *Human Resource Development Review*, *7*(1), 3–12. https://doi.org/10.1177/1534484307311804

Wigfield, A., & Eccles, J. S. (2000). Expectancy-Value Theory of Achievement Motivation. *Contemporary Educational Psychology*, *25*(1), 68–81. https://doi.org/10.1006/ceps.1999.1015

8
The Future Digital Scholar

Wim Van Petegem

In this chapter we focus on

✓ The future, and how a digital scholar can prepare for it.

✓ Agility as a specific characteristic of an ever-evolving digital scholar.

✓ Action research as an activity for a digital scholar to evolve in the right direction.

✓ Trend watching in order for a digital scholar to somehow be able to predict what comes next.

✓ Leadership taken by digital scholars as change agents.

Keywords: Agile methods; action research; trend watching; leadership; change management

8.1 Introduction

"Prediction is very difficult, especially if it is about the future." With this quotation Nils Bohr, Nobel laureate in Physics (1922), wanted to say that it is maybe easy to find a model explaining a certain phenomenon based on evidence or data available at that moment, but that it is quite another matter to identify those characteristics or features of the model which will be similar or valid in the future as well. So far in this book we have focused on a framework reflecting our stance on how a digital scholar should or could behave and evolve in the current digital world. This is based on our own personal experiences, what we know from our own research, and what we learnt through many training opportunities we have given in the past about this topic. In that respect we didn't take a purely scientific viewpoint on digital scholarship, but followed a more pragmatic approach, though still keeping the academic context in mind. When we now want to expand our view and look into the future, we are on slippery ice. We can imagine a couple of things that might affect our lives as digital scholars in the coming years, just looking at evolutions in the digital world with regard to technology, to pedagogy, to academic leadership, etc. No one however could foresee the impact on our lives, private and professional, of a tiny virus causing the COVID-19 pandemic. Is that important? Yes and no. It is good to have some certainties in life, as they give some predictability to what comes next. On the other hand, we should learn to cope with the ever faster changing world around us.

In this chapter we want to equip the reader with some guidelines on how to deal as a digital scholar with the future and the changes that are sure to come our way. We present them in the form of recommendations and use active verbs to express our belief that we all should actively take our future in our hands. Critically consider these and use them to your advantage. We hope they help you better understand how to move around in the Digital Scholar framework, to take your position and further evolve as a Digital Scholar, now and in the future.

8.2 Be agile

8.2.1 Agile methods
Agile methods are best known from the world of software engineering or software project development, where they have taken over from the traditional waterfall and later spiral models. In the waterfall model a huge software project is broken down into a linear sequence of smaller phases, each one corresponding to a set of ordered specific tasks and depending on the deliverables of the previous phase. An improved way of developing huge software projects was called the spiral model, originally described by Boehm, B. (1988). The process is now described as cyclic, in which each cycle is a sequence of steps (like in the waterfall model), but cycles are expanding, from smaller to larger steps, covering more and more elements of the project and coping with more and more risks associated with the project (including costs). More recently agile methods have been introduced. The principles of agile methods are popularised in an Agile manifesto[63], published in 2001. The advantage of agile methods is clearly that they permit one to respond to rapid changes in the context or feedback from end users or customers, without spending too many resources on tight plans. 'Just enough' planning and delivering smaller, but more frequent, intermittent results allow us to assemble quick feedback and integrate that into future plans at a minimum cost. And above all, agile methods are about people: human interaction, collaboration with customers and team mates prevail above procedures, processes and super-detailed documentation.

8.2.2 Agile methods for a digital scholar: Focusing on instructional design

In instructional design we could detect a similar tendency, from more rigid and linear ways of thinking to more agile approaches. Without going into too much detail, we will present basically two models at both ends of the spectrum.

The most linear model commonly used in course or curriculum development is called the ADDIE model. This model was created in 1975 by the Centre for Educational Technology at Florida State University for the U.S. Army. It describes the different steps of instructional design as a cyclic sequence of an <u>A</u>nalysis, <u>D</u>esign, <u>D</u>evelopment, <u>I</u>mplementation and <u>E</u>valuation phase.

Figure 8.1 The ADDIE model for instructional design.

In the analysis phase, you pre-plan and think about the goals, the audience, the learning objectives, the context, the constraints, etc. Next, you design the course on paper, i.e., you write a sort of storyboard for the course (naming the learning units, identifying contents, writing the instructions, etc.). In the development phase, you really build, produce and/or assemble learning materials. And, then, you begin teaching the course, in interaction with your students. At the end, you look back and reflect on the outcomes, from the viewpoint both of the students and your own learning experience.

There has been ample criticism of this model, mainly for its simplicity and its rigidity. Variations have been proposed, with smaller feedback loops or shortcuts in the cycle. Alternatively, totally different approaches have been introduced like, e.g., the 4C-ID model by van Merriënboer et al. (2002)

at the end of the 1990s. Four C (4C) stands for four components, and ID for instructional design. The basic claim is that four interrelated components are essential and need to be designed properly in blueprints for complex learning: (a) learning tasks, (b) supportive information, (c) just-in-time (JIT) information, and (d) part-task practice. It is valuable to take note of such models, but it is beyond the scope of this book to go into much more detail here.

Clearly, ADDIE and even 4C-ID have been developed long before agile and other iterative processes have been introduced. Due to the successful implementation of these agile methods in other disciplines (e.g., software engineering), similar attempts have been made in instructional design thinking as well. One such model, proposed by Allen Interactions Inc., is called SAM (Successive Approximation Model).[64] It consists of three main phases: preparation, *iterative* design, and *iterative* development. First, in the preparation phase all the information and background knowledge relevant to the project is gathered, with all stakeholders involved and with a focus on alignment between learning needs and learning solution. This process is done quickly and called "savvy start". Second, in the iterative design phase, all design, prototyping and review rotates iteratively in small steps. Proto-typing is a vital part in the design phase. A prototype or mock-up makes conceptual ideas more visible for the team members, instead of describing and listing all the design specifications on paper. Finally, in the iterative development phase, the project team members rotate through development, implementation and evaluation. Design proof, the product of the first cycle, is made at the beginning of the development phase. After presenting and testing the design proof, an alpha version is released, and then it evolves to a beta version before finally rolling out the gold version. Not too many authors have already described their experiences with this model of instructional design. Though, for sure, it has potential, and it comes closer to con-temporary ways of development and collaborative teamwork. With proven success in the world of software development, it fits very well into the digital world that scholars as teachers can benefit from.

And what about scholars as agile researchers? In a career column in Nature, Pirro (2019) describes how agile methods can be applied in a PhD research project. The protocol involves the following steps: splitting the work (in smaller layers of activities, each with tangible results), sprint planning (with supervisor and any other stakeholder), sprint execution (i.e., work-ing on a specific task for a limited amount of time), weekly scrum (short meeting with the supervisor), sprint review, retrospective and planning (to discuss results, expectations and changes), and go back to the first step. The approach has been tested in the case of running a set of experiments, but also in writing a manuscript or building a simulation code. Among the benefits are faster knowledge development, fewer misunderstandings about research expectations, increased output and improved motivation and morale. Needless to emphasise that such an agile research mindset goes very well together with twenty-first century skills and digital competencies. In case you want to probe further, you can find more inspiration in Kucirkova and Quinlan's (2017) work.

One particular example of agility in research concerns citizen science. It is a way in which citizens participate in scientific research projects by observing, gathering or processing data themselves, depending on their personal interest, time and technological resources. The digital scholar involved in such research projects needs to be able to use the proper digital technologies, and above all needs to have an agile mindset to interact with the citizens. Indeed, it is first of all important to select a technology that fits the research objectives, is user-friendly and is affordable for a large share of the envisaged population so that the participants can easily report their findings with the (academic) researcher. It is equally important, however, for a digital scholar to interact sincerely with the 'assistant' researchers: listening to their concerns and expectations, helping them with the tools, replying to their questions, finetuning or adjusting the research methods according to their needs and capabilities, stimulating quality and rigour in the process, persuading them to persevere when it becomes challenging, communicating about the results, involving them in future actions, etc. A genuine interest in how members of the community can contribute to real scientific experiments, each one according to their own ability, is a *conditio sine qua non* for a successful citizen science project. It must be clear that in this case an agile digital scholar is not just a teacher, even not merely a researcher, but someone who is also heavily competent for outreach activities, science communication and community service, the third pillar of academic life.

8.3   Watch the trends

Sometimes we hear people complain that whenever they have learnt about a new skill or a new tool, it is outdated before they can ever start using it. What is, then, the added value of putting effort into learning new things all the time? Or, more constructively, how can you know what will be important in the future so you can better select what to focus on or prepare for? There is no definite answer to these questions, but it certainly helps to famil-

163

iarise yourself with trend reports made by others. Indeed, it is not necessary, if not impossible, to do your own foresight research and explore possible or probable futures yourself. Other parties are better placed, better equipped and better financed to set up these studies in a scientifically correct way. We present here a few of these trend reports and trend-watching instruments as an example for the future digital scholar to find his or her way in the multitude of information and documentation openly and publicly available or not. Plenty of other documentation has been published on trends in teaching and learning in higher education. It is beyond the scope of this book to go into much more detail. The selection below is therefore to be seen purely as an illustration that could be inspirational for future digital scholars, if only because it is based on a (semi-)scientific basis and published by a trustful organisation. We invite the reader to become acquainted with these resources but always handle them with the necessary academic critical attitude.

8.3.1 Gartner hype cycle

The Gartner hype cycle is a branded graphical presentation developed and used by the American research, advisory and information technology firm, Gartner, to represent the maturity and adoption of technologies and applications, and how they are potentially relevant for exploiting new opportunities.

The hype cycle can be divided into five key phases of a technology's life cycle:

✓ **Innovation Trigger**: A potential technology breakthrough, public demonstration, product launch or other event kicks things off. Often no usable products exist yet and broad-scale or long-term viability is still unproven.

✓ **Peak of Inflated Expectations**: Early publicity produces a number of success stories, and a wave of 'buzz' is built up – often accompanied by scores of failures. Some institutions take action; many do not.

✓ **Trough of Disillusionment**: Interest wanes as experiments and implementations fail to deliver. Missed expectations (e.g., problems with performance, slower-than-expected adoption) lead to disillusionment. Providers can survive only when they improve their products to the satisfaction of early adopters.

✓ **Slope of Enlightenment**: Some early adopters overcome the initial hurdles, begin to experience benefits and recommit efforts to move forward. Institutions draw on the experience of the early adopters. Their understanding grows about where and how the innovation can be used to good effect and, just as importantly, where it brings little or no value.

- ✓ **Plateau of Productivity**: Mainstream adoption starts to take off. The technology's broad applicability and relevance are clearly paying off.

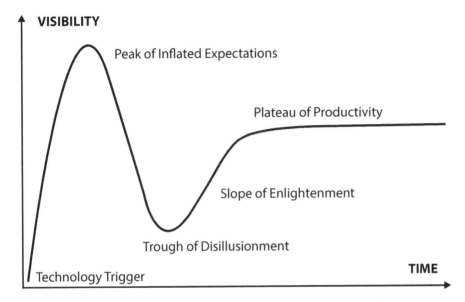

Figure 8.2 The general Gartner Hype Cycle for the adoption of technology ("Gartner Hype Cycle", by Jeremy Kemp, licensed under the Creative Commons Attribution-Share Alike 3.0 Unported).

Although there are numerous criticisms of the hype cycle (e.g., not scientific in nature, not a 'cycle', no precise definitions for emotions like disillusion and enlightenment, etc.), it is nevertheless worthwhile keeping the 'cycle' in mind when one gets excited about a hyped new technology or tool. Especially if you soon discover it is not the ultimate solution to all problems and needs to persevere in order for one finally to understand its real potential… this is not abnormal, and you are not alone!

Each year Gartner publishes a hype cycle for emerging (digital) technologies. They plot each technology on the curve where it is supposed to be in the hype cycle. Other organisations or institutions use the same curve for technologies specifically related to education. It would be interesting to compare historical plots and to check whether these (learning) technologies really have lived up to their original promise and have achieved a 'plateau' of maturity in their usage in higher education institutes.

8.3.2 EDUCAUSE Horizon Report

A well-known report on trends in teaching and learning, especially focusing on (the use of) learning technologies, is the annual Horizon Report,[65] originally published since 2002 by the now defunct New Media Consortium, but currently by EDUCAUSE. This report profiles key trends and emerging technologies and practices shaping the future of teaching and learning and envisages a number of scenarios and implications for that future. While in the past the report was oriented towards 'time-to-adoption' (i.e., technological trends, and later also barriers and enablers, in the next coming two, four and six years), the current report begins now with a scan of the actual situation and offers more evidence and data to build upon four scenarios for the future of teaching and learning. They include an optimistic "growth" scenario and a realistic "constraint" scenario, a pessimistic "collapse" scenario and an imaginative "transformation" scenario. In order to collect 'signals' and 'impacts' for trends, the foresight methodology of the IFTF (Institute for the Future) is used, i.e., the STEEP framework: <u>S</u>ocial, <u>T</u>echnological, <u>E</u>conomic, <u>E</u>ducational, and <u>P</u>olitical trends are identified. These larger trends are then used by a panel of experts from across the higher education landscape, who proceeded their work through a modified Delphi method. They were tasked with responding to and discussing a series of open-ended prompts, as well as participating in subsequent rounds of consensus voting, all based on their own expertise and knowledge. This methodology ensures that the panel's future forecasts are sufficiently grounded in 'real' data and trends and are not merely science fiction. Nevertheless, it would be interesting to look back in history and compare the predictions of previous years with what actually occurred. Since the publishers have changed the methodology for the 2020 edition of the report as described above, this might be a bit tedious at this point, but wait a few years...

It is maybe worthwhile to delve a little bit deeper into the Delphi method, especially when applied in a digital age. The Delphi method was originally invented by the RAND Corporation in the 1950s. It was a structured communication and collaboration mechanism to gain consensus, synthesise opinion and process feedback from experts. Needless to say, in those times this research process was constructed within the limited possibilities of the available technology. With the advent of digital tools, the previous limitations for participation, time for response and processing, and geographical location no longer restricted the application of a Delphi method in scientific research. Moreover, in today's digital age, researchers have access to technological tools for conducting Delphi studies that extend beyond these limitations, thus providing both opportunity and challenge to conduct global studies, automate elements of the research process, and handle greater amounts of data in shorter time frames. Indeed, using online communication, collaboration and survey tools helps the Delphi researcher to prepare the study, design surveys, communicate with participants, analyse data (both qualitative and quantitative), protect against researcher bias and manage other mistakes. More practical considerations can be read in the *Handbook of Research on Innovative Techniques, Trends, and Analysis for Optimized Research Methods* | IGI Global (igi-global.com), chapter 9: Delphi Method in a Digital Age: Practical Considerations for Online Delphi Studies, by Christine A. Haynes and Kaye Shelton (pages 132-151).[66]

8.3.3 *Innovating Pedagogy*
A similar report, but starting from a totally different perspective, i.e., from a pedagogical point of view rather than the technology, is the annual Innovating Pedagogy[67] report published by the Open University's Institute of Educational Technology (UK), in collaboration with the National Institute for Digital Learning at Dublin City University (Ireland). By 'innovative pedagogies' the authors mean novel or changing theories and practices of teaching, learning and assessment for the modern, technology-enabled world. The process followed by the researchers has involved sharing ideas, discussing innovations, reading research papers, reports and blogs, and commenting on each other's draft contributions. They worked together to compile their report by long-listing new educational concepts, terms, theories and practices, then reducing these to ten top ones that have the potential to provoke major shifts in educational practice. And, lastly, the authors drew on published and unpublished writings to compile ten sketches of new (innovative) pedagogies that either already influence educational practice or might transform education in the future. An interesting remark made by the authors concerns the diversity of the readership across the world. It forces them to examine carefully assumptions made about how innovations that originate in one place may be perceived elsewhere. This approach creates added value to the report, not always true for other similar trend reports.

8.4   Engage in action research

As a future digital scholar, it is recommended that you research your own practices, in collaboration with others, and do that in a systematic and formal way. This could be done through 'action research', i.e., taking the action, researching the action and learning from the process. Therefore, an apparent characteristic of action research is that you do it for yourself, i.e., to improve your own personal behaviour as a digital scholar. Several authors[68] have described how to implement action research as a project *by* teachers *for* teachers in a classroom, working together with students and colleagues. We rely on their practical advice, and try here, where possible, to generalise their ideas to all activities of a digital scholar.

Action research can be approached as a real research project. The basic process consists of the following steps:

- ✓ Planning stage:
    - Identify and limit the topic; this could be based on your own interest or something that you like to examine in depth, something that you like to improve or correct, something with a sufficiently narrow focus and feasible to do within boundary constraints of time, skills, budget, etc.
    - Gather information, by e.g., talking to colleagues, skimming manuals, checking websites, bringing up ideas, etc.
    - Review the related literature (books, journals, websites etc.) in depth, to make an informed and scientifically sound decision on the further steps to take, and (later) to connect existing theory with the actual practice.
    - Develop a research plan, from stating the research question (best is to state only one in order to keep focus), formulating the hypotheses, identifying possible variables, choosing the proper methodology, to selecting and/or developing the research instruments, while taking into account the issue of research ethics.
- ✓ Acting stage:
    - Implement the plan and collect the data, through observation, query, survey or study, using appropriate digital tools whenever possible and appropriate.
    - Analyse the data, both quantitative and qualitative (in action research mostly both types of data are necessary), with proper statistical methods and triangulation processes.
- ✓ Developing stage:
    - Develop an action plan, based on your findings, with short-term and modest objectives, in order to take small steps in improving your current practice.
- ✓ Reflecting stage:
    - Share and communicate the results, with your peers at your own institution, but also with the broader community, e.g., through

presenting at a local or global conference, writing a scientific paper in a peer reviewed journal, etc.
– Reflect on the research process and try to adapt wherever needed for a next cycle.

In most cases, these steps are taken in a cyclic and iterative manner. Some of the steps may be skipped or rearranged, if appropriate.

Such action research can be used effectively to bridge the gap between theory and practice, and to expand the knowledge base on digital scholarship. In that way, all your academic (and professional) skills as a teacher and researcher will be tapped in and will help to conduct the action research in a correct way, from the ideation up to the reflection phase. Needless to say, digital tools can and will help you to conduct the action research at all stages, and by now you should be able to know how to use them to your own benefit.

8.5   Lead the change

The Technology Acceptance Model (TAM), as described by Davis, F.D. (1989), claims that "perceived ease of use (PEOU)" (the degree to which a person believes that using a particular technology would be free from effort) and "perceived usefulness (PU)" (the degree to which a person believes that using a particular system would enhance his or her job performance) are the two fundamental determinants of user acceptance of new technology.

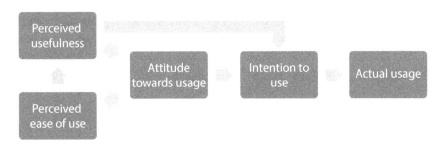

Figure 8.3 The Technology Acceptance Model.

The author further states that when users find a technology 'easy to use', then they perceive it also as a 'useful' one, or: PEOU influences PU. TAM offers the causal relationships of these two fundamental constructs (PEOU and PU) with three other constructs, "attitude toward usage (ATT)", "behavioural intention to use (BI)" and "actual usage (AU)". ATT is defined as an individual's positive or negative feeling about using a certain technology. According to TAM, both PEOU and PU influence ATT, i.e., if users find a technology useful and easy to use then they develop a positive attitude towards this technology. BI is defined as the degree to which a person plans to perform or not perform some specified future behaviour. TAM claims that, if users find a specific technology a useful one (PU), then they develop a positive intention of using it. Similarly, users' positive attitude to a specific technology (ATT) leads them developing an intention to use this technology. So, both PU and ATT directly influence BI. TAM further suggests that users' behavioural intention (BI) shapes their actual use of the technology (AU). If users have the intention to use a specific technology, then they will use it.

The basic version of this technology acceptance model, as described above, has been frequently used in many situations, also in the academic world (e.g., to model take up of learning technologies in education). Nevertheless, it has been widely criticised for several reasons. Newer versions (refined, adopted or expanded) have been developed better to define the terminology and to include more factors, like e.g., the Unified Theory of Acceptance and Use of Technology (Venkatesh et al. (2003)). It is beyond the scope of this book to go into detail here. We just want to emphasise that it is possible to describe the process steps taken by a digital scholar from seeing some potential in a certain new digital technology up to actually using this technology in your scholarly work. We need a change in mindset, in attitude to technology and in behaviour of using it (or not).

Not all digital scholars look at change in the same way. The process of adoption over time of a new technology (or innovation in general) is typically illustrated by the technology adoption lifecycle, represented as a classical normal distribution or "bell curve". The model indicates that the first group of people to use a new technology is called "innovators", followed by "early adopters". Next come the early majority and late majority, and the last group eventually to adopt a technology are called "laggards" or "phobics".

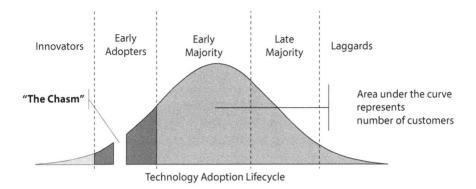

Figure 8.4 The Technology Adoption Lifecycle ("The Technology Adoption Lifecycle", by Craig Chelius, licensed under the Creative Commons Attribution 3.0 Unported).

✓ *Innovators* – These are risk-oriented, leading-edge minded individuals who are extremely interested in technological developments. Innovators are a fractional segment of the overall population.

✓ *Early Adopters* – A larger but still relatively small demographic, these individuals are generally risk-oriented and highly adaptable to new technology. Early adopters follow the innovators in embracing new products; they tend to be younger and more technology savvy.

✓ *Early Majority* – Much larger and more careful than the previous two groups, the early majority are open to new ideas but generally wait to see how they are received before adopting them.

✓ *Late Majority* – Slightly conservative and risk-averse, the late majority is a large group of potential users who need to be convinced before jumping into something new.

✓ *Laggards* – Extremely frugal, conservative and often technology-averse, laggards are a small population of usually older and technology averse individuals who avoid risks and want to embrace new ideas only when they are forced to.

The most difficult step is making the transition between early adopters and the majority, indicated by 'the chasm' in the picture. It is the moment when the hype turns into more moderate and mainstream considerations when adopting a certain technology (cf. the Gartner hype cycle), or the moment where enough momentum has been built in order for a technology to become a standard.

As a digital scholar, you can position yourself on the curve, based on the way you feel about adopting new technologies in your scholarly work. We leave it up to the reader to make that exercise by themselves. Your position might also depend on the technology itself: for some products produced by your preferred manufacturer you might feel tempted to be on the left side of the curve, while for products from competitors or less hyped in the media you need a bit more encouragement to try them out.

One particular interpretation of the technology adoption life cycle is seeing it as a model to grow, moving from right to left over the bell curve. With increasing digital competences, a scholar once afraid of new technologies can become a more and more digital scholar and eventually belong to the bigger majority or, why not, to the early adopter or even innovator category. Fortunately, you don't have to make the moves all by yourself. You can rely on the help of change agents.[69] Change agents in this context are people who are advocating the growth and adoption of an innovation. In the higher education world, they are those who are doing new things in their scholarly work in the institution and trying to spread those ideas outwards. In a way this is just what scholars should do: investigating new things and diffusing their findings in an influential manner among people. It helps that the change agents are digital scholars themselves: they can translate in a culturally sensitive way the message of innovation such that it gets the best chance of being favourably received by as many as possible other still doubting colleagues. As a digital scholar you probably have the proper competences to succeed in this challenge. There is maybe one attribute that deserves special attention here, and this is 'power', not in the sense of hierarchical or managerial control, but rather the possession of knowledge and the ability to pass that on and exert enough influence to make changes for the better (i.e., innovate). That transforms future digital scholars into leaders of change. They will be able to read the signs of the times, to keep their institutions agile to respond to new trends, and to initiate changes whenever needed.

In order to help future digital scholars in taking up this role as a leader, we present here a useful framework called FIRRST by Cavanagh et al. (2018), which is an acronym describing the following set of principles to make strategic decisions:

- ✓ **F**ollow the Energy: identify pockets of opportunity where critical mass is forming, capitalise on those "rising tides" of institutional energy, and direct them to organisational goals.
- ✓ **I**nvent the Future: recognise potential opportunities, have the courage and fortitude to envisage a future that does not yet exist, inspire others to see this vision and keep the organisation moving towards that vision even amid inevitable setbacks.

✓ **R**esearch and Make a Decision: involve pilots or even formal research studies (e.g., action research), gather as much data as possible (and needed), and don't be afraid of making a decision even with insufficient data.

✓ **R**ecognise Resource Limitations: allocate the available resources in the chosen direction, mobilise partners or extra resources, and don't forget to include the creative potential and passion of all involved as a valuable resource.

✓ **S**olve the Big Problems: embed the innovation into the broader institutional challenges and strategic goals.

✓ **T**ake Action: recognise a window of opportunity, eliminate risks to a sufficient extent and accept others, choose the proper time to decide and act!

This FIRRST framework can serve as a practical heuristic for future digital scholars making decisions for themselves and leading the change in their institutions.

8.6   In sum: Go DIGITAL

With the above recommendations in mind, all that remains for a future digital scholar is to take the final step, and really go digital. In order to help, and to stimulate any scholar to engage in the digital world or, even better, to shape this digital world, we give some extra advice in the form of a few active verbs:

✓ **D**are! Don't wait, don't hesitate, take your chance, don't have cold feet, jump or dive into the deep, take the risk, be adventurous, go for it!

✓ **I**gnite! Start right away, enlighten your environment, inspire your peers, encourage colleagues, instigate new ideas, light the fire!

✓ **G**row! Broaden your scope, rise to the top, push the limits, expand across borders, mature and become wiser, increase your impact!

✓ **I**nteract! Don't hide, network with partners, build a community, participate and communicate, connect with like-minded people, cherish relationships!

✓ **T**ry! Experiment and explore new things, practise, give it a chance, don't give up, back off to blow up better, don't reinvent the wheel!

✓ **A**ppeal! Fascinate, attract, charm, please, invite, engage, be stunning, show your best (digital) side!

✓ Learn! Treasure your successes, turn mistakes into learning opportunities, stand on the shoulders of giants, integrate new knowledge, be wise, keep smiling!

This list does not pretend to be complete, and for sure you can find other and more active verbs to be a scholar teaching and researching in the digital world of today and tomorrow. "The best way to predict the future is to create it!" That statement was true when Abraham Lincoln, 16th President of the United States, first said it, and even more true today, when the world is a whole lot less predictable than it used to be. With our Digital Scholar framework as basis and with the above recommendations to evolve we hope to have given some pointers on how to do that as a digital scholar in the future. Safe journey!

References

Boehm, B (1988). A Spiral Model of Software Development and Enhancement. *IEEE Computer*. 21 (5): 61–72. doi:10.1109/2.59. S2CID 1781829

Cavanagh, T.B. & Thompson, K. Keeping (2018), FIRRST Things First: The Delicate Dance of Leading Online Innovation at Your Institution, in *Leading and Managing e-Learning*; Piña, A.A., Lowell, V.L. & Harris, B.R. (eds.); Part of the Educational Communications and Technology: Issues and Innovations book series (ECTII) Springer, pp. 1-12

Davis, F. D. (1989). Perceived usefulness, perceived ease of use, and user acceptance of information technology. *MIS Quarterly*, Vol. 13, No. 3 (Sept. 1989), pp. 319–340, Stable URL: https://www.jstor.org/stable/249008

Kucirkova, N. & Quinlan, O. (2017), eds. *The Digitally-Agile Researcher*, https://www.mheducation.co.uk/the-digitally-agile-researcher-9780335261529-emea-group McGraw Hill

Pirro, L. (2019) *How agile project management can work for your research*, https://www.nature.com/articles/d41586-019-01184-9, (19 April 2019)

Van Merriënboer, J., Clark, R., & De Croock, M. (2002). Blueprints for Complex Learning: The 4C/ID-Model. *Educational Technology Research and Development*, 50(2), 39-64. Retrieved December 23, 2020, from http://www.jstor.org/stable/30221150

Venkatesh, Viswanath; Morris, Michael G.; Davis, Gordon B.; Davis, Fred D. (2003). "User Acceptance of Information Technology: Toward a Unified View". MIS Quarterly. 27 (3): 425–478. doi:10.2307/30036540

Notes

1   See: http://www.vliruos.be/en/about-us/.

2   See: www.sun.ac.za/ada.

3   https://www.merriam-webster.com/dictionary/affordance.

4   See; https://ec.europa.eu/jrc/en/digcomp/digital-competence-framework.

5   See: https://ec.europa.eu/jrc/en/digcompedu.

6   See: https://digitalcapability.jisc.ac.uk/.

7   Wikipedia contributors. (2021, April 27). Scholar. In *Wikipedia, The Free Encyclopedia*. Retrieved 18:51, May 24, 2021, from https://en.wikipedia.org/w/index.php?title=Scholar&oldid=1020117766.

8   See: https://ec.europa.eu/jrc/en/science-update/new-digcomp-report-develops-proficiency-levels.

9   www.futurelearn.com.

10   See Chapter 5, section 5.2.1 to discover more about cumulative knowledge building.

11   See Steve Wheeler discussing his technical audio and video creation setup at http://www.steve-wheeler.co.uk/2020/10/technical-requirements.html.

12   The ideas in this section draws on the collaborative webinar *Using audio as a teaching tool, for student engagement and assessment* that was delivered in 2020 as part of our Emergency Remote Teaching (ERT) series of professional learning opportunities. I want to thank and acknowledge my colleagues from the Division for Learning and Teaching Enhancement, Stellenbosch University, for their ideas that inspired this audio focus on assessment, namely Sonja Strydom, Nicoline Herman, Gerda Dullaart and Jean Farmer.

13   www.storycenter.org.

14   See https://www.jotform.com/blog/best-voice-recording-software/ for a list of top audio recording software.

15   Otter – https://otter.ai; Cleanfeed – www.cleanfeed.net.

16   To see 31 podcasting services and the top 7 (which offer some free usage) go to https://www.podcastinsights.com/best-podcast-hosting/. In fact, go to www.podcastinsights.com anyway, for a very extensive introduction to all aspects of podcasting!

17   See Chapter 2: *The Evolving Digital Scholar as Author.*

18   See Chapter 3: *The Evolving Digital Scholar as Storyteller.*

19   TED is a non-profit organisation, which started in 1984 as a multidisciplinary conference. According to its website, the organisation is 'devoted to spreading ideas, usually in the form of short, powerful talks (18 minutes or less)'. The video-recorded talks can be accessed at https://www.ted.com/talks, although the organisation has broadened its multimedia production capacities to a range of popular audio podcast channels as well.

20 We elaborate more on this iterative process of engagement and networking in Chapter 6: *The Digital Scholar as Networker*.

21 A quick Internet search of 'open source and freely available software for [video/audio/infographic/other multimedia] editing' will generate a multitude of options. Most institutions or organisations have licences for basic multimedia authoring software, and you can contact a relevant Information Technologies or support staff member to enquire. Alternatively, you can use the software installed on your smart device. Most laptops and smartphones have basic video, audio and visual design tools installed, with multiple 'How to' videos available about each software on the Internet.

22 'Audience' here refers to any group of people that is expected to engage with the relevant digital artefact. Such an audience can be a student cohort, colleagues, clients, scholars in a similar field, fellow researchers collaborating on a project, a broader sector of interested members of the public, or a more literal audience at a conference or workshop – to name but a few.

23 To articulate these three overlapping contexts, the author of this chapter, Miné de Klerk, has developed a simple framework, the 'Digital Content Creation for Scholars'. It was developed based on her research on the process of instructional design in an online and hybrid higher education context.

24 We refer here not only to the ability to go beyond the channelisation and aggregation of content, but rather the skill to select, evaluate and sort through digital artefacts in order to open up opportunities for further knowledge production (Dallas 2016).

25 [Add list of entry-level of video software – or link to an appendix?].

26 The 'Digital Scholar as Networker' chapter expands more on how such formative feedback data can be accessed – even for smaller or individual projects.

27 See: https://www.loom.com/.

28 See: https://miro.com/.

29 See: https://www.easel.ly/.

30 www.merriam-webster.com. This does not point to the more technical concept of *digital integration* that ensures that "platforms, applications, systems and interfaces are integrated" and that data must "flow from one application to another" (Oblinger, 2014, p.30).

31 Also known as VLE (Virtual Learning Environments) in some parts of the world.

32 www.legitimationcodetheory.com has a wealth of information on the different dimensions of the toolkit as well as an extensive searchable knowledgebase.

33 We want to acknowledge our colleagues, Marcia Lyner-Cleophas and Ilse Erasmus, from Stellenbosch University's Special Needs Office, for helping us "see" this side of the educational technology world and for introducing me to the basic concepts and scholarship on which this section is built.

34 CAST is one of the important starting points to find out more about the UD4L framework as well as the UD4L Guidelines – www.cast.org. Also see the seminal works of

Anne Meyer, David Rose and David Gordon (Meyer, Rose, & Gordon, 2014) and Sheryl Burgstahler (Burgstahler, 2015) on the subject.

35 See www.telerik.com/blogs/web-accessibility-guidebook-for-developers for a very concise and usable overview of digital UD4L principles and practices.

36 See https://www.w3.org/WAI/test-evaluate/preliminary/ for a comprehensive but not overwhelming overview and resources.

37 E.g., the free Web Accessibility training course developed by Google in partnership with Udacity: https://www.udacity.com/course/web-accessibility--ud891.

38 The companies' websites give in-depth information and support around this theme: *Apple*: www.apple.com/uk/accessibility/; *Microsoft*: www.microsoft.com/en-gb/accessibility/; and *Adobe*: www.adobe.com/accessibility.html.

39 The Microsoft office 365 package offers an Accessibility Checker in Word and PowerPoint e.g., as well as options in Outlook to request responders to an e-mail to use accessibility principles. Adobe's powerful PDF reader and editor also has the ability to check for accessibility and all the examples above also guide the user to remedy the in-accessible elements with practical suggestions.

40 www.creativecommons.org.

41 Some of the well-known archives are: (a) https://www.oercommons.org/; (b) https://www.oerafrica.org/; (c) The University of Pittsburgh OER Big List of resources https://pitt.libguides.com/openeducation/biglist_and (d) MOM – George Mason University OER Metafinder service https://oer.deepwebaccess.com.

42 Explore the world of MOOCs by going to www.mooc-list.com.

43 OPM – Online Programme Management, a phenomenon that emerged in higher education where for-profit companies design, develop, advertise for, enrol and even offer courses and programmes etc. on behalf of universities.

44 Access the DeLTA framework process and resources at www.sun.ac.za/english/learning-teaching/ctl/t-l-resources/design-for-learning-teaching-and-assessment-(delta)-cycle.

45 The ABC Learning Design Toolkit can be accessed at www.abc-ld.org.

46 All Gilly Salmon's digital design approaches, like Carpe Diem, e-Tivities, the Five-stage Model of online learning, as well as e-Moderation, can be accessed at www.gillysalmon.com. It is worth the visit!

47 The *Visualisation tools* can be explored at: LAMS (Learning Activity Management System) – www.lamsinternational.com, WebCollage – https://www.gsic.uva.es/webcollage/, CADMOS (Courseware Development Methodology for Open instructional Systems) – https://www.cloudwatchhub.eu/cadmos-personal-learning-tool-graphical-personalisation, and CompendiumLD – http://compendium.open.ac.uk/download/download.htm.

48 The *Pedagogical planners* can be explored at: DialogPlus – http://edutechwiki.unige.ch/en/DialogPlus_Toolkit, Phoebe – http://www.phoebe.ox.ac.uk/, and The Learning Designer – http://learningdesigner.org.

49   See, e.g., Chapter 4 Section 4.5.3.

50   AHEEN – www.aheen.net.

51   To experience the webinars, please go to www.adunlearn.net and click on the AHEEN Augmented Webinars link.

52   www.jove.com.

53   www.openstax.org.

54   Asynchronous engagement occurs online, but not in 'real time'. A typical example is an online forum where users can post comments any time, and the online discussion can therefore unfold at everyone's own pace.

55   https://dictionary.cambridge.org/dictionary/english/networking.

56   https://www.merriam-webster.com/dictionary/networking.

57   We refer, more specifically, to structural social network analysis. This kind of research focuses on the social relationships linking individuals rather than on the individuals themselves (Freeman, 2004).

58   See Chapter: *The Digital Scholar as Author: Choices in disseminating scholarly work.*

59   Networked Participatory Scholarship is similar to open social scholarship, in terms of both activities' use of digital, networked technologies to facilitate collaborative scholarship. Networked Participatory Scholarship, however, is not necessarily completely open – it can also include smaller online communities and private blog groups. Although the case for open scholarship is made in this book and certainly forms part of the networking approach argued for in this chapter, we choose to refer to Networked Participatory Scholarship here as an umbrella term for the collaborative, often non-traditional scholarly communication practices that can still be applied to contemporary social networking approaches.

60   Chapter 2: 'The Evolving Digital Scholar as Author' provides another, complementary perspective on academic social networking sites, and how these platforms can serve as an opportunity to move beyond journal publication towards a digital context.

61   Much has been written about the application of social media to support student learning and the various pedagogical affordances of open, digital networks. For the purposes of this chapter, however, we focus less on networking as a means for student-teacher communication. Rather, the type of networking we refer to is one where the digital scholar engages with fellow teaching practitioners, in order develop professionally, to evolve their pedagogical approach and even to engage in the scholarship of teaching and learning.

62   http://blog.online.colostate.edu/blog/online-education/moocs-101-a-beginners-guide-to-free-online-courses/.

63   See: http://agilemanifesto.org/.

64   See: Allen Interactions: The SAM Model for eLearning Development, Agile Instructional Design available at: https://www.alleninteractions.com/services/custom-learning/sam/elearning-development.

65 You can find the link to the latest Horizon Report 2020 here: https://library.educause.edu/resources/2020/3/2020-educause-horizon-report-teaching-and-learning-edition.

66 Book available at: https://www.igi-global.com/gateway/book/187112.

67 You can find a link to the latest Innovating Pedagogy report here: http://www.open.ac.uk/blogs/innovating/.

68 See e.g.: You and Your Action Research Project – Jean McNiff – Google Books_and Action Research: Teachers as Researchers in the Classroom – Craig A. Mertler – Google Books.

69 See: Breaking the Mold: An Educational Perspective on Diffusion of Innovation/Change Agents and Education – Wikibooks, open books for an open world.

About the authors

Wim Van Petegem holds an MSc degree in Electrical Engineering from the University of Ghent (Belgium), an MSc degree in Biomedical Engineering from the KU Leuven (Belgium) and a PhD degree in Electrical Engineering from KU Leuven (1993). He worked at the University of Alberta, Edmonton (Canada), at the Open University of the Netherlands and at the Leuven University College (Belgium). From 2001 until 2012 he was the head of the Media and Learning Centre and later he became Director of the Teaching and Learning Department at KU Leuven (Belgium). Currently he is Professor at the Faculty of Engineering Technology at KU Leuven. His research interests are in learning technologies, instructional design, engineering education, hyflex learning and digital scholarship. He is teaching courses on professional and intercultural engineering skills and implements innovative approaches to teaching and learning in other courses. He is a regular panel member of review committees to assess the quality of education in Flanders and the Netherlands. He is actively involved in different international networks of universities (like SEFI, EDEN and MEDEA), and he is heavily engaged in development cooperation projects with the Global South. He also gives regularly training sessions (in Leuven and abroad, e.g., in South Africa, Ecuador, Ethiopia, China, Philippines, etc.) on innovation in education and digital competences for teachers and professional support staff.

JP Bosman is Director of the Centre for Learning Technologies (CLT) at Stellenbosch University (SU), South Africa. He trained and taught in the field of Theology at SU before becoming involved in academic development work. After working at the Centre for Teaching and Learning at SU as well as a start-up educational software company, he became Head and later Director of the CLT, a Centre that spearheads and supports SU's strategies for the use of ICT in Learning and Teaching. His teaching and research interests are around instructional and learning design, blended and hybrid learning, m-learning literacy, graduate attributes, the digital scholar, teaching in the digital world and, more recently, the Scholarship of Educational Leadership. He currently lives in Cape Town with his wife, two children and two cats.

Miné de Klerk is the Hybrid Learning Project Manager at Stellenbosch University (SU), South Africa. She is responsible for the strategic management of SU's expanding portfolio of hybrid and online offerings, in order for the university to meet the evolving needs of adult learners. She holds a Master's Degree in Business Administration (MBA) and BA(Hons) from the University of Cape Town. At the time of writing for this book, she is also a Ph.D. candidate (Higher and Adult Education), researching traditional universities' shift to online teaching and learning through the lens of complex systems thinking. Her research foci further include the facilitation of dialogic engagement in the virtual classroom.

Sonja Strydom is a Deputy Director (Academic Development & Research) at the Centre for Learning Technologies and a Research Fellow at the Centre for Higher and Adult Education and Stellenbosch University. She holds a PhD in Education from the University of Stellenbosch and a DLitt et Phil in Psychology from the University of South Africa. Sonja teaches on a number of short and postgraduate higher education courses at Stellenbosch University, regionally and internationally. Her current research interest is in the field of digital-mediated curriculum development, digital pedagogies and well-being and alternative research methodologies in furthering the field of higher educational research.

www.ingramcontent.com/pod-product-compliance
Lightning Source LLC
LaVergne TN
LVHW012335060326
832902LV00012B/1890